GW01048784

ECLECTIC INTEGRATION IN COUNSELLING AND PSYCHOTHERAPY

Edited by

Windy Dryden and

John C. Norcross

GALE CENTRE PUBLICATIONS 1990 ISBN 1 870258 11 8

First published in The British Journal of Guidance and Counselling, Vol
17 no 3, September 1989. Hobsons Publishing PLC, Cambridge.

Published by Gale Centre Publications
Whitakers Way
Loughton, Essex
IG10 1SQ

British Library Cataloguing in Publication Data
Eclecticism and integration in counselling and
    psychotherapy.
    1. Psychology. Psychotherapy
    I. Dryden, Windy II. Norcross, John C.
    616.8914

ISBN 1 870258 11 8

Printed in Great Britain by BPCC Wheatons Ltd, Exeter

CONTRIBUTORS

Dr John C. Norcross
Department of Psychology, University of Scranton, Scranton, Pennsylvania 18510, USA.

Dr Arnold A. Lazarus
Graduate School of Applied and Professional Psychology, Rutgers University, PO Box 819, Piscataway, NJ 08855, USA.

Dr Bernard D. Beitman
Department of Psychiatry, University of Missouri, Clinic 6, 1 Hospital Drive, Columbia, Missouri 65212, USA.

Dr Stanley B. Messer
Graduate School of Applied and Professional Psychology, Rutgers University, PO Box 819, Piscataway, NJ 08855, USA.

CONTENTS

INTRODUCTION

Eclecticism and Integration in Counselling and Psychotherapy: Introduction

Windy Dryden

Department of Psychology, Goldsmiths' College, University of London

John C. Norcross,

Department of Psychology, University of Scranton, USA

As Norcross and Grencavage note in their paper, between one-third and one-half of North American counsellors and psychotherapists identify themselves as eclectics or integrationists. While corresponding figures for non-American practitioners are not available, it is likely that the movement away from single-school approaches to counselling and psychotherapy is occurring worldwide. For example, the Society for the Exploration of Psychotherapy Integration (SEPI) - an interdisciplinary organisation for professionals interested in eclectic and integrative psychotherapy - has members in Argentina, Australia, Austria, Belgium, Canada, Italy, Japan, the Netherlands, Norway, Portugal, Sweden, the United Kingdom, Uruguay and West Germany. The UK branch of SEPI, for example, has held two national conferences with future ones planned.

And yet, much of the writing on eclectic and integrative approaches to counselling and psychotherapy appear in journals and edited volumes published in North America. There is even an entire journal devoted to this area - the *Journal of Integrative and Eclectic Psychotherapy* - again published in America. The purpose of this book is to introduce current thinking in this exciting and rapidly developing field to British readers.

First, Norcross and Grencavage provide an overview of the field of eclecticism and integration in counselling and psychotherapy, defining key terms, discussing potential obstacles to psychotherapy integration and describing emerging themes that are currently being debated.

It is important to recognise that the field of eclecticism and integration is still in an early state of development and different authorities have different views. In this context, Lazarus and Beitman put forward their different ideas and state why they identify themselves with technical eclecticism and common factor integration respectively.

Finally, Messer adds some cautionary notes and expands on the theme of obstacles that practitioners face on the path towards integration and eclecticism first introduced by Norcross and Grencavage. According to Messer, such obstacles exist in three realms of endeavour - the therapeutic relationship, the constitution of knowledge, and visions of reality.

The field of eclecticism and integration in counselling and psychotherapy is currently marked by three characteristics: optimism, lively debate and, to a lesser extent, caution. It is our opinion that the following papers clearly demonstrate these characteristics and thus give an accurate picture of a field at an exciting stage of development.

CHAPTER 1

Eclecticism and Integration in Counselling and Psychotherapy: Major Themes and Obstacles

John C. Norcross and Lisa M. Grencavage

Department of Psychology

University of Scranton, USA

The movement to integrate the psychotherapies has experienced dramatic and unprecedented growth in the past decade. This article overviews the integration movement, beginning with a confluence of mutually reinforcing factors which have fostered its development. The three main modes of the movement - technical eclecticism, theoretical integration, and common factors - are critically reviewed. Recurrent obstacles to psychotherapy integration are then considered, including territorial interests of 'pure systems' therapists, the paucity of empirical research, and absence of a common language. Finally, six emerging themes that characterise eclecticism and integration are presented: complementarity; convergence; systematic practice; prescriptive matching; an empirical base; and the long view.

A metamorphosis is occurring in mental health (London, 1988; Moultrup, 1986): the integration of the psychotherapies. This movement has experienced dramatic and unprecedented growth in the past decade (Beitman *et al.*, 1989). Consider the following pieces of evidence - like exhibits introduced into a court of law - to support the assertion that eclecticism and integration are here to stay and merit our attention:

Exhibit A: Between one-third and one-half of all American psychotherapists now identify themselves as eclectics (e.g. Beitman *et al.*, 1984; Garfield and Kurtz, 1974; Jayaratne, 1982; Norcross *et al.*, 1989; Perlman, 1985; Peterson *et al.*, 1982; Prochaska and Norcross, 1983; Smith, 1982; Watkins *et al.*, 1986), making it the modal theoretical orientation of clinicians. If you are forced to guess a colleague's persuasion, then guess eclecticism.

Exhibit B: Several interdisciplinary psychotherapy organisations devoted to rapprochement and integration have been formed in the past ten years. Prominent among these are the Society for the Exploration of Psychotherapy Integration (SEPI) and the International Academy of Eclectic Psychotherapists (IAEP).[1]

Exhibit C: The National Institute of Mental Health (NIMH) sponsored a workshop on research in psychotherapy integration (Wolfe and Goldfried, 1988), because of their belief 'that treatments of greater efficacy, efficiency, and safety will result from efforts to integrate the best elements from different schools of psychotherapy. In addition, research on integrated treatment models may lead to the development of a comprehensive model of psychotherapy process that will have solid empirical backing.'

Exhibit D: The founding of an international quarterly - the *Journal of Integrative and Eclectic Psychotherapy* - explicitly devoted, for the first time, to the systematic synthesis of therapeutic methods, theories, and/or formats.[2]

Exhibit E: The publication of at least 50 books, by our count, on synthesising various counselling concepts and techniques. These volumes range from attempts to meld two theories of psychotherapy - such as Wachtel's (1977) benchmark *Psychoanalysis and Behavior Therapy* - through acclaimed systems of eclectic practice - such as Lazarus's (1976; 1981; 1985) *Multimodal Therapy* - to compilations of prescriptive treatments - such as Frances *et al.*'s (1984) *Differential Therapeutics in Psychiatry.*

2

Exhibit F: Examination of a number of leading counselling textbooks (Brabeck & Welfel, 1985) reveals a growing trend to identify their theoretical perspective as eclectic. Authors explicitly state that counsellors must adapt an eclectic stance based on mounting research, a relativistic perspective to 'truth', the individuality of the practitioner, and the uniqueness of the client.

Exhibit G: As one final piece of evidence, a recent panel of psychotherapy experts predicted that eclecticism would increase in popularity more than any therapy system in the forthcoming decade (Prochaska and Norcross, 1982).

In this article we overview the burgeoning movement to integrate the psychotherapies. We will begin with the historical origins of the movement and consider the modes of integration. Recurrent obstacles to, and emerging themes of, the movement are then reviewed. Our focus is primarily on synthesising counselling methods and theories; neither the combination of psychotherapy and psychopharmacology, nor the synthesis of therapeutic formats (e.g. individual, family, group) are addressed here.

Origins of the movement

Eclecticism as a point of view has probably existed as long as philosophy and psychotherapy. The third-century biographer, Diogenes Laertius, referred to an eclectic school which flourished in Alexandria in the second century AD (Lunde, 1974). In psychotherapy, Freud consciously struggled with the selection and integration of diverse methods (Frances, 1988). More formal ideas on synthesising the psychotherapies appeared in the literature as early as the 1930s (French, 1933).

Although the notion of integrating various therapeutic approaches has intrigued mental health professionals for some time (Goldfried, 1982; Goldfried and Newman, 1986), it has been only within the past 15 years that integration has developed into a clearly delineated area of interest. The last decade, in particular, has witnessed both a general decline in ideological struggle and the stirrings of rapprochement. The debates across theoretical systems appear to be less polemical, or at least more issue-specific. The theoretical substratum of each system is undergoing intensive reappraisal, as psychotherapists acknowledge the inadequacies of any one system and the potential value of others.

A confluence of scientific, professional, and socio-economic circumstances produced the recent preoccupation with psychotherapy integration. Five intertwined, mutually reinforcing factors have fostered the movement in the past decade (Beitman *et al.*, 1989; Goldfried and Newman, 1986; London, 1983; 1988; Norcross, 1986).

(1) Proliferation of therapies. Psychotherapy systems appear and vanish with bewildering rapidity on the diffuse, heterodox scene. In the late 1950s, Harper (1959) identified 36 distinct systems of psychotherapy. In the mid-1970s, Parloff (1976) discovered over 130 therapies on the market-place, or more appropriately, the 'therapeutic jungleplace.' In the mid-1980s, Karasu (1986) reported a count of more than 400 presumably different 'schools' of psychotherapy. The proliferation of therapies has been accompanied by a deafening cacophony of rival claims. The result has been variously characterised as confusion, fragmentation, and discontent (Norcross, 1986).

In describing the genesis of scientific revolutions, Kuhn (1970) found that the abandonment of any given paradigm is ordinarily preceded by a period of 'crisis.' This crisis is characterised by the open expression of discontent about the current state of affairs and by the proliferation of different orientations. The field of psychotherapy, it would appear, is currently experiencing such a pre-paradigmatic crisis (Goldfried and Padawer, 1982).

The field has been staggered by over-choice and fragmented by future shock. Which of 400 plus therapies should be studied, taught, or bought? No single theory has been able to corner the market on validity or utility. London (1988, pp. 5-6) wryly observed that the hyperinflation of brand name therapies has produced narcissistic fatigue. 'With so many brand names around that no one can recognize, let alone remember, and so many competitors doing psychotherapy, it is becoming too arduous to launch still another new brand.'

(2) Inadequacy of single theories. A related factor is the growing consensus that no one approach is clinically adequate for all problems, patients, and situations. Beutler (1983) suggests that the proliferation of theories is both a cause and symptom of the problem - that neither the theories nor the techniques are adequate to deal with the complexity of psychological problems. Clinical realities have come to demand a more flexible, if not integrative, perspective.

Psychotherapy has entered a period of intense self-examination in which the failures of our pet theories are reappraised and their limitations realised. The grand systems era has been undermined by a wave of scepticism in which leading figures of each school have criticised their own theories and assumptions. Omer and London (1988) trace scepticism within psychoanalysis (e.g. implausibility of truly 'free associations', doubts about Freud's archaeology metaphor), behaviour therapy (e.g. questions on presumed derivation from learning theory, over-reliance on observed behaviours), and cognitive therapy (e.g. doubts on the precedence of cognition over affect and behaviour, difficulty of dispelling dysfunctional thinking). Obviously, no clinical theory has a monopoly on truth or utility.

The integration movement, to some extent, reflects dissatisfaction with single approaches. Surveys of self-designated eclectic and integrative clinicians have revealed that their alignment is motivated in part by disillusionment with single therapy systems (Garfield and Kurtz, 1977; Norcross and Prochaska, 1988). Indeed, very few counsellors adhere tenaciously to a single therapeutic tradition (Larson, 1980; Smith, 1982).

(3) Equality of outcomes. Despite a noticeable increase in the quantity and quality of psychotherapy research, it has not been possible to show that one therapeutic approach is clearly superior to another (see e.g. Bergin and Lambert, 1978; Frank, 1979; Landman and Dawes, 1982; Smith *et al.*, 1980). There are few conditions in which the therapy system leads to differential success in

5

outcome, and with few exceptions, there is little compelling evidence to recommend the use of one type over another in the treatment of specific problems. Luborsky *et al.* (1975) borrowing a phrase from the Dodo bird in *Alice in Wonderland*, concluded that 'everybody has won and all must have prizes'. Or, in the words of London (1988, p.7): 'Meta-analytic research shows charity for all treatments and malice towards none'.

A paradox has emerged from the equivalence conclusion: no differential effectiveness despite technical diversity (Stiles *et al.*, 1986). A number of resolutions to this paradox have been advanced, including the unspecificity of outcome measurement, the poor integrity of treatments, and the elucidation of common core factors in the therapist, client, or alliance. The two most common responses seem to be a specification of factors common to successful treatments and a synthesis of useful concepts and methods from disparate therapeutic traditions.

(4) Search for common components. The identification of common change processes or therapeutic factors has been called the most important psychotherapy trend in the 1980s (Bergin, 1982). Strupp (1973; 1982) has noted that the significant advances in psychotherapy research have resulted from better conceptual analyses of basic processes operating in all forms of therapy rather than from premature comparisons of techniques. This observation stems from the emerging view that the commonalities in all forms of therapy are far more impressive than their apparent differences. A transtheoretical analysis of prominent psychotherapy systems demonstrated how much therapeutic systems agree on the processes producing change while disagreeing on the content to be changed (Prochaska, 1984).

Frank (1973; 1982) posited that all psychotherapeutic methods are elaborations and variations of age-old procedures of psychological healing. The features that distinguish psychotherapies from each other, however, receive special emphasis in our pluralistic and competitive society. Since the prestige and financial security of counsellors hinge on their particular approach being more successful than that of their rivals, little attention has traditionally been accorded to the identification of shared components.

Frank, among others, has argued that therapeutic change is predominantly a function of factors common to all approaches: an emotionally charged, confiding relationship; a healing setting; a rationale or conceptual scheme; and a therapeutic ritual. For Garfield (1980), these common factors entail the relationship, catharsis, explanation, reinforcement, desensitisation, information, and time. Similarly, Karasu (1986) identified three non-specific change agents that all therapy schools share: affective experiencing, cognitive mastery, and behavioural regulation. These authors have noted that features shared by all therapies account for an appreciable proportion of clinical improvement, and psychotherapy outcome research has generally substantiated this claim (Lambert, 1986). Ironically, 80% of the psychotherapy literature is devoted to specific technologies and procedures, which account for only 10%-12% of change (Beutler, 1986).

(5) Socio-economic contingencies. A fifth and final reason for integrating the psychotherapies is a matrix of social, political, and economic influences. The total therapy industry continues to grow: invasion of non-doctoral and non-medical counsellors, the boom in professional practice, the mushrooming of training institutes, and the outpouring of third-party funding in the States (London, 1988).

Meanwhile, pressures are mounting in the United States from insurance companies, government policy-makers, consumer groups, and judicial officials for accountability. Third-parties and the public are demanding crisp and informative answers regarding the quality, durability, and efficiency of psychosocial treatments (Parloff, 1979). Until recently the field has had the luxury of functioning within a culture of individual professional freedom. Clinical services had been in steady demand in the market-place, generally oblivious to economic forces and socio-political realities. However, the shrinking job market, in-

7

creased competition, and diminishing public support portend a future discontinuous with our expansive past (Fishman and Neigher, 1982).

Without some change from the field, psychotherapists stand to lose prestige, customers, and money. These socio-political considerations have Americans increasingly pulling together rather than apart. Mental health professionals report that the impact of political and economic changes have led them to work harder, to be more creative, and to adjust their treatments to meet the needs of their clients (Brown, 1983). Intertheoretical co-operation and a more unified psychotherapy community represent attempts to respond to these socio-political forces. As the external demands escalate, so too will the spirit of open inquiry and therapeutic integration.

Modes

Three main thrusts have become evident in the contemporary movement to integrate the psychotherapies: (1) technical eclecticism; (2) theoretical integration; and (3) common factors (Arkowitz, 1989). The common factors approach, as previously mentioned, seeks to determine the core ingredients different therapies might share in common, with the eventual goal of developing more efficacious treatments based on these components. The long considered 'noise' in psychotherapy research is being reconsidered by some as the main 'signal' elements of treatment (Omer and London, 1988).

One way of determining common therapeutic principles is by focusing on a level of abstraction somewhere between theory and technique. This intermediate level of abstraction, known as a clinical strategy, may be thought of as a heuristic that implicitly guides the efforts of experienced therapists. Goldfried (1980, p. 996) argues:

'To the extent that clinicians of varying orientations are able to arrive at a common set of strategies, it is likely that what emerges will consist of robust phenomena, as they have managed to survive the distortions imposed by the therapists' varying theoretical biases.'

Common factors may, in fact, be the curative factors.

Some observers have argued that the concentrated study of commonalities across theoretical orientations may prove premature or unproductive (cf. Allport, 1968; Haaga, 1986; Henle, 1986; Messer, 1983; 1986a; Messer and Winokur, 1980; 1984; Norcross, 1981; Wilson, 1982). For one, different therapies embody alternative visions of life with different basic possibilities of human existence and growth. These are not easily subjected to integration or consensus. For another, the common factors - or non-specific - approach is a way of thinking, not a way of conducting therapy. One cannot do 'nothing specific' in therapy or training. For still another, commonalities identified to date may be so superficial - radically different in substance, structure, and intent - as to make clinical strategies analogous to broad descriptive classification. The category of 'fruit' is surely a superordinate category of both apples and oranges, but their comparisons might not be particularly useful. As such, commonalities not only fail to provide much direction for training and therapy but also provide inadequate guidelines for research. Messer expounds on these and other trade-offs in his article in this book on 'Integration and Eclecticism in Counselling and Psychotherapy: Cautionary Notes'.

The preponderance of clinical practice and professional contention resides, however, in the distinctions between eclecticism and integration. How do they differ? Which is the more fruitful strategy for knowledge acquisition and clinical practice?

The NIMH Workshop (Wolfe and Goldfried, 1988) and two recent studies (Norcross and Napolitano, 1986; Norcross and Prochaska, 1988) have clarified this question. Table 1 summarises the consensual distinctions between eclecticism and integration.

Table 1: **Eclecticism v. integration**

Eclecticism	Integration
Technical	Theoretical
Divergent (differences)	Convergent (commonalities)
Choosing from many	Combining many
Applying what is	Creating something new
Collection	Blend
Selection	Synthesis
Applying the parts	Unifying the parts
Atheoretical but empirical	More theoretical than empirical
Sum of parts	More than sum of parts
Realistic	Idealistic

The definition of eclecticism parallels the dictionary meaning: 'choosing what is best from diverse sources, styles, and systems'; 'using techniques and rationales based on more than one orientation to meet the needs of the individual case'; 'the systematic use of a variety of therapeutic interventions in the treatment of a single patient'; and 'the pragmatics of selecting a variety of procedures and wider interventions for specific problems'. The common thread is that technical eclecticism is relatively atheoretical, pragmatic, and empirical.

Lazarus (1967; 1977; 1984), the most eloquent proponent of technical eclecticism, uses procedures drawn from different sources without necessarily subscribing to the theories that spawned them, whereas the theoretical integrationist draws from diverse systems which may be epistemologically or ontologically incompatible. For Lazarus and other technical eclectics, no necessary connection exists between metabeliefs and techniques. It is not necessary to build a composite from divergent theories, on the one hand, nor to accept divergent conceptions, on the other, in order to utilise their technical procedures. 'To attempt a theoretical rapprochement is as futile as trying to picture the edge of the universe. But to read through the vast amount of literature on psychotherapy, *in search of techniques*, can be clinically enriching and therapeutically rewarding' (Lazarus, 1967, p. 416). Lazarus advances this argument in more detail in his article 'Why I am an Eclectic (Not an Integrationist)' in this book.

Theoretical integration, by small contrast, refers to a commitment to a conceptual or theoretical creation beyond a technical blend of methods. This creation is described as 'an articulated framework or roadmap', 'superordinate umbrella', 'new, conceptually superior theory', and 'a coherent and continually evolving theoretical framework'. It is theoretical, idealistic, and, for now at least, less empirical. In his article elsewhere in this book, 'Why I am an Integrationist (Not an Eclectic)', Beitman advances a synthetic perspective based on theoretical integration and common factors.

To reiterate: the primary distinction is that between empirical pragmatism and theoretical flexibility. Or to take a culinary metaphor (cited in Norcross and Napolitano, 1986, p. 253): 'The eclectic selects among several dishes to constitute a meal, the integrationist creates new dishes by combining different ingredients.'

The net result of this differentiation is that the term 'eclecticism ' is restricted in use to the technical, atheoretical combination of methods. The term 'integration' denotes the conceptual synthesis of diverse theoretical systems. We hasten to add that the goals of both eclectics and integrationists are similar indeed, although their means may diverge. In clinical practice, however, the distinction is largely semantic and conceptual, not particularly functional. Moreover, the two strategies are not as distinct as they may appear: no technical eclectic can totally disregard theory and no theoretical integrationist can totally ignore technique.

Recent research demonstrates an emerging preference for both the term 'integration' and the practice of theoretical integration, as opposed to technical eclecticism. Results of these two studies (Norcross and Napolitano, 1986; Norcross and Prochaska, 1983) show clinicians preferring the self-identification of integrative over eclectic by almost a two to one margin. That is, they like the ring of 'integrative' better than "eclectic'. In similar fashion, when instructed to select the type of integration they practice, the majority of eclectics - 61% and 65% - chose theoretical integration.

The preference for integration over eclecticism probably represents a historical shift. In a 1975 investigation (Garfield and Kurtz, 1977), most favoured eclecticism; in our 1986 study (Norcross and Prochaska, 1988), most favoured integration. This may reflect a theoretical progression analogous to a social progression: one that proceeds from segregation to desegregation to integration. Eclecticism has represented desegregation, in which ideas, methods, and people from diverse theoretical backgrounds mix and intermingle. Currently we appear to be in transition from desegregation to integration, with increasing efforts directed at discovering viable integrative principles for assimilating and accommodating the best that different systems have to offer.

This, then, summarises *how* counsellors are integrating - the method. Let us now turn to *what* they integrate - the content.

The short and simple answer is 'everything' - counsellors are mixing and mingling techniques, theories, and formats from every theory ever promulgated. The longer and more complex answer is shown in table 2. Here, eclectic psychologists rated their frequency of use of six theories in clinical practice. The ratings formed a matrix of 15 possible, non-redundant combinations; the nine most frequent are presented in table 2. *All* possible combinations were selected by at least one respondent. A cognitive-behavioural integration was the most common, followed closely by humanistic-cognitive and psychoanalytic-cognitive syntheses. Interestingly, the cognitive revolution in psychotherapy is making its impact known here: the three most popular combinations all involve cognitive theory.

Table 2: **Most frequent combinations of theoretical orientations**

Combination	1986 %	Rank	1976* %	Rank
Cognitive and behavioural	12	1	5	4
Humanistic and cognitive	11	2		
Psychoanalytic and cognitive	10	3		
Behavioural and humanistic	8	4	11	3
Interpersonal and humanistic	8	4	3	6
Humanistic and systems	6	6		
Psychoanalytic and interpersonal	5	7		
Systems and behavioural	5	7		
Behavioural and psychoanalytic	4	9	25	1

* Percentages and ranks were not reported for all combinations in the 1976 study (Garfield and Kurtz, 1977).

The synthesis of theories and techniques is assuredly part of the integration movement. But what about the combination of therapy formats - individual, family, group - and the combination of medication and psychotherapy? In both cases, a strong majority of clinicians - 80% plus - considered these to be within the legitimate boundaries of integration (Norcross and Napolitano, 1986). Of course, the inclusion of psychopharmacology enlarges the scope to integrative treatment, rather than integrative psychotherapy per se.

These findings underscore the obvious: eclecticism comes in many guises and manifestations. It is clearly not a monolithic entity or a single operationalised system. To refer to the eclectic or integrative approach falls prey to the 'uniformity myth' (Dryden, 1984; Kiesler, 1966).

Conspicuously absent from our discussions are the more conventional, pure-form (or brand name) therapy systems, such as behavioural and psychoanalytic therapy. Do these contribute to the integrative and eclectic movements? No, in the narrow sense of not creating a paradigm for synthesising various interventions and conceptualisations. But yes, in the broader and more important sense of adding to our therapeutic armamentarium and enriching our understanding of the clinical process. One cannot integrate what one does not know.

Recurrent obstacles

The accelerated development of eclectic and integrative psychotherapies has not been paralleled by serious consideration of their potential obstacles and trade-offs (Arkowitz and Messer, 1984; Dryden, 1986). If we are to avoid uncritical growth or fleeting interest in eclectic/integrative psychotherapy, then some honest recognition of the barriers we are likely to encounter is sorely needed (Goldfried and Safran, 1986). Caught up in the excitement and possibilities of the movement, we have neglected the problems - the 'X-rated topics' of integration. Healthy maturation, be it for individuals or for movements, requires self-awareness and constructive criticism.

What's stopping psychotherapy integration now? Norcross and Thomas (1988) conducted a survey of the Society for the Exploration of Psychotherapy Integration (SEPI) membership to answer this question. Fifty-eight prominent integrationists rated, in terms of severity, twelve potential obstacles using a five-point, Likert-type scale. The top five obstacles and their mean scores are presented in table 3.

Table 3: **Obstacles to psychotherapy integration**

	Severity rating	
Obstacle	Mean	Rank
Intrinsic investment of individuals in their private perceptions and theories	3.97	1
Inadequate commitment to training in more than one psychotherapy system	3.74	2
Approaches have divergent assumptions about psychopathology and health	3.67	3
Inadequate empirical research on the integration of psychotherapies	3.58	4
Absence of a 'common' language for psychotherapists	3.47	5

1 = not an obstacle; 3 = moderate obstacle; 5 = severe obstacle.

The most severely rated obstruction centred around the partisan zealotry and territorial interests of 'pure'-form psychotherapists. Representative responses here were: 'egocentric, self-centered colleagues'; 'the institutionalisation of schools'; and 'ideological warfare, factional rivalry'. In examining the history of different therapy methods, Goldfried (1980, p. 991) notes that, traditionally, therapists have been guided by a particular theoretical framework, 'often to the point of being completely blind to alternative conceptualisations and potentially effective intervention procedures'.

Unfortunately, professional reputations are made by emphasising the new and different, not the basic and similar. In the field of psychotherapy, as well as in other scientific disciplines, the ownership of ideas secures far too much emphasis. Although the idea of naturally-occurring, co-operative efforts among professionals is engaging, their behaviour, realistically, may be expected to reflect the competition so characteristic of our society at large (Goldfried, 1980).

Inadequate training in eclectic/integrative therapy was the second-ranked impediment. The reasons are multiple and explicable. Training students to competence in multiple theories and interventions is unprecedented in the history of psychotherapy. Understandable in the light of its exacting and novel nature, the acquisition of integrative perspectives has occurred quite idiosyncratically and perhaps serendipitously to date.

The critical training question is how to facilitate adequate knowledge of and competence in the various psychotherapeutic systems. On the one hand, intense concentration on a single theoretical system, though possibly myopic and misleading, is often secure and complete. Cursory exposure to multiple therapeutic systems, on the other hand, leaves students with a few clichés and disunited techniques, though it does encourage integration (Norcross,1986; Robertson, 1986). Three special sections of the JIEP have addressed integrative training and supervision (Beutler *et al.*, 1987; Halgin, 1988; Norcross *et al.* 1986).

The third-ranked obstacle concerned differences in ontological and epistemological issues. These entail basic and sometimes contradictory assumptions about human nature, determinants of personality development, and the origins of psychopathology. For instance, are people innately good, evil, both, neither? Do phobias represent learned maladaptive habits or intrapsychic conflicts? But it may be precisely these diverse world views that make psychotherapy integration interesting, in that it brings together the individual strengths of these complementary orientations (Beitman *et al.*, 1989).

We have not conducted sufficient research on psychotherapy integration - the fourth obstacle to be addressed here. Comparative outcome research has been a limited source of direction with regard to selection of method and articulation of prescriptive guidelines. If our empirical research has little to say, and if collective clinical experience has divergent things to say, then why should we do A, not B? We may again be guided by selective perception and personal preference, a situation the integrative movement seeks to avoid.

A seemingly intractable obstacle to the establishment of clinically sophisticated and consensually validated integrative psychotherapies is the absence of a common language (Norcross, 1987). This was rated the fifth most serious impediment to progress. Each psychotherapeutic tradition has its own jargon, a clinical shorthand among its adherents, which widens the precipice across differing orientations (Goldfried and Newman, 1986).

The 'language problem', as it has become known, confounds understanding of each other's constructs and, in some cases, leads to active avoidance of those constructs. Many a behaviourist's mind has wandered when case discussions turn to 'transference issues' and 'warded-off conflicts'. Similarly, psychodynamic therapists typically tune out buzz words like 'conditioning procedures' and 'discriminative stimuli'. Isolated language systems encourage clinicians to wrap themselves in semantic cocoons from which they cannot escape and which others cannot penetrate. As Lazarus (1986) concluded: 'Basically, integration or rapprochement is impossible when a person speaks and understands only Chinese and another converses only in Greek!' (p. 241).

A common language thus offers the promise of increased communication between clinicians and researchers, on the one hand, and among practitioners of diverse persuasions, on the other. Meaningful transtheoretical dialogue may allow us to enrich each other's clinical practices, access the empirical literature, and discover robust therapeutic phenomena cutting across varying orientations (Norcross, 1987).

The purpose of a common language is to facilitate communication, comprehension, and research. It is not intended to establish consensus. Before an agreement or a disagreement can be reached on a given matter, it is necessary to ensure that the same phenomenon is in fact being discussed. Punitive superego, negative self-statements, and poor self-image may indeed be similar phenomena, but that cannot be known with certainty until the constructs are defined operationally and consensually (Stricker, 1986).

To be sure, this is a demanding task (Messer, 1987). In the short run, using the vernacular - descriptive, ordinary, natural language - might suffice (Driscoll, 1987). In the long run, a common language may profit from being linked to a superordinate theory of personality or derived from an empirical data base (e.g. Ryle, 1987; Strong, 1987).

Emerging themes

(1) Complementarity. Clinical experience and research findings alike lead us to the conclusion that each therapeutic orientation has its share of failures, and that none is consistently superior to any other. These observations have stimulated many workers in the field to suggest that contributions from orientations other than their own might be fruitfully employed. The weakness of any one perspective might be complemented by another's strength. Pinsof (1983, p. 20), for example, describes his integrative problem-centred therapy as one that 'rests upon the twin assumptions that each modality and orientation has its particular domain of expertise, and that these domains can be interrelated to maximize their assets and minimize their deficits'.

In considering the potential strengths and liabilities of an integrative approach, patient variables will probably play the central role in determining the most appropriate therapeutic intervention (Beitman *et al.*, 1989). Treatment decision rules have been advanced for a number of patient variables: verbal and introspection skills, stage of change, reactance and defensive style, and breadth of psychopathology (e.g. Beitman, 1987; Beutler, 1983; Fensterheim, 1983; Prochaska and DiClemente, 1984; Wachtel, 1987).

This, then, is the important first step: to view rival systems not as an adversary, but as a healthy diversity (Landsman, 1974); not as contradictory, but as complementary (Norcross, 1986). We can begin to build rather than burn the bridges which span chasms separating theories. At long last, perhaps we can temper our splitting propensities and reject our puerile claims of 'We are good - they are bad' (Miller, 1985) and proudly exclaim 'We are good - they are also good' (Norcross, 1988).

(2) Convergence. There is a pernicious misconception in our field that certain processes and outcomes are the exclusive property of particular therapy systems. Norcross (1988) labelled this fallacy the 'exclusivity myth'. Cases in point are the behaviourist's contention of exclusive ownership of behaviour change, the experientialist's presumed monopoly on intense affective expression, and the psychoanalyst's assertion of unique genetic insights. The exclusivity myth is part and parcel of the hostile, ideological cold war. The profession has encountered a proliferating number of therapies - each purportedly superior with regard to some disorder or clientele.

Fortunately, amid this strife and bewilderment, a therapeutic 'underground' has slowly emerged (Wachtel, 1977). Though not associated with any particular school and not detailed in the literature, the underground reflects an unofficial consensus of what experienced clinicians believe to be true.

Many observers (Goldfried, 1982; Karasu, 1977; Marmor,1980; Messer, 1986b) have noted increasing confluence of attitudes and practices amongst the psychotherapies. Moreover, recent studies of clinical practitioners point to many areas of convergence as well as remaining points of contention. In one study (Mahoney *et al.*, 1989), 486 clinical psychologists representing five major theoretical orientations responded to 40 standardised questions about optimal practices in psychotherapy. The results indicated considerable transtheoretical convergence on the importance of novel exploratory activity, self-examination, and self-development in psychotherapy. Behaviourists rated psychological change as significantly less difficult than did their colleagues of other persuasions unless they had been in psychotherapy themselves. In another study (Friedling *et al.*, 1984), 85 psychodynamic and 110 behavioural psychologists reported on their use of operationally-defined therapy activities. Over one-half of these methods were used by both groups, 15% were mutually rejected, and only 29% were employed exclusively by members of either orientation.

Unfortunately, the early research is based on what counsellors *say* they do rather than on direct observations of what they *actually* do or, more importantly, what their clients experience them as doing. Nonetheless, there does appear to be a contemporary tendency to grow alike, to develop similarities in form. These areas of convergence, moreover, may well reflect robust phenomena that stand a good chance of being related ultimately to successful therapy outcome (Goldfried and Safran, 1986; Lambert, 1986).

(3) Systematic practice. The term 'eclecticism' has acquired an emotionally ambivalent, if not negative, connotation for some clinicians due to its alleged disorganised and indecisive nature. In some corners, eclecticism still connotes undisciplined subjectivity, 'muddle-headedness', the 'last refuge for mediocrity, the seal of incompetency', or 'a classic case of professional anomie' (quoted in Robertson, 1979). Dryden (1984) observes that many of these psychotherapists wander around in a daze of professional nihilism experimenting with new 'fad' methods indiscriminately. Indeed, it is surprising that so many clinicians admit to being eclectic in their work, given the negative valence the term has acquired (Garfield, 1980).

This unsystematic eclecticism is primarily an outgrowth of pet techniques and inadequate training. It is eclecticism 'by default', lacking sufficient competence for an integrated approach and selecting interventions on the basis of subjective appeal. Eysenck (1970, p. 145) characterises this haphazard form of eclecticism as a 'mish-mash of theories, a hugger-mugger of procedures, a gallimaufry of therapies', having no proper rationale or empirical evaluation.

The emergent trend is to view integration in its many guises as systematic (Norcross and Prochaska, 1988). A product of painstaking clinical research and theoretical work, systematic integration is necessarily 'by design': that is, clinicians competent in several therapeutic systems who select interventions based on clinical experience and research findings. The strengths of systematic integration lie in its ability to be taught, replicated, and evaluated. Rotter (1954, p. 14), years ago, summarised the matter as follows: 'All systematic thinking involves the synthesis of pre-existing points of view. It is not a question of whether or not to be eclectic but of whether or not to be consistent and systematic.'

(4) Prescriptive matching. Maslow once remarked that if you only have a hammer you treat everything like a nail. The history of psychotherapy has repeatedly confirmed this observation. Sad to say, the preponderance of contemporary clinicians probably still reach for their favourite tool when confronted with puzzling or unsettling cases. It is not uncommon for our inveterate colleagues to recommend the identical treatment - their treasured proficiency - to virtually every patient who crosses their paths (Norcross, 1985).

The integration movement asks clinicians to become discriminating craftworkers who selectively draw on experience and research to meet the multi-varied challenges of clinical reality. Discriminating clinicians go beyond subjective preference, institutional custom, and immediate availability to predicate their treatment selection on patient need and comparative outcome research. That is, they develop and employ an expanded toolbox instead of senselessly 'hammering away' at anything remotely similar to a nail.

The challenge is to enhance the optimal match between patient and treatment. This process has been assigned various names - differential therapeutics (Frances *et al.*, 1984), treatment matching (Beutler, 1983), dispositional assignment (Beutler and Clarkin, in press), prescriptive psychotherapy (Goldstein and Stein, 1976). But the goal is identical: to improve the efficacy, applicability, and efficiency of psychotherapy by tailoring it to the unique needs of the client. The question is no longer 'Does it work?' Rather, the question has become 'Does it work best for this client?' Answers to this query will probably place the client's welfare above the counsellor's theoretical narcissism.

Prescriptionism is concerned with that elusive, empirically driven match among patient, disorder, and treatment. With increasing refinement in the categorisation of disorders and more precise delineation of change strategies, further advantages of prescriptive treatments may be found. At that point, effective therapy will be 'defined not by its brand name, but by how well it meets the need of the patient' (Weiner, 1975, p. 44).

(5) Empirical base. The reader may understandably protest: how do we consensually determine 'what works best' given our divergent ontological and epistemological assumptions? The question is less problematic for technical eclectics who meld techniques separate from their 'theoretical baggage' but it remains a thorny issue for integrationists trying to synthesise entire theories. Adams (1984, p. 92) pointedly inquires how clinicians settle their differences: 'by negotiation, kissing and making up, taking a vote, or gathering data?'

Our preference is for gathering empirical data. Clinicians and researchers alike have long called for the development of psychotherapies with a strong empirical base. An empirical base for practice has at least two meanings (Fischer, 1986). The first is the use of research to inform practice, as in the selection of clinical techniques and interpersonal stances; the second is in the careful, objective evaluation of the effects of the psychotherapies. The latter is particularly urgent as there is little unambiguous evidence of the clinical superiority of an integrative approach over existing systems (Yates, 1983). It is important to note, though, that the reverse is true as well (Wachtel, 1983).

We need to discover, in functional terms, which therapist behaviours and treatment strategies are more effective with which types of clients (Cross and Sheehan, 1981; Paul, 1967). In this respect, a natural affinity exists between process research and psychotherapy integration (Beutler and Clarkin, 1989; Goldfried and Safran, 1986; Wolfe and Goldfried, 1988). 'Bottom up' research strategies (i.e. descriptive and exploratory investigations, both clinical and empirical, at the level of actual therapeutic practice), especially those which investigate process-outcome linkages, can unearth the mechanisms of therapeutic change and develop a cumulative body of knowledge regarding the process of change. Process-outcome linkages can thereby contribute to all three of the current thrusts of the integrative movement - by stimulating theory (theoretical integration), by identifying effective methods for that disorder and that client (technical eclecticism), and by delineating transtheoretical elements (common factors).

Several years ago the senior author and a colleague (Norcross and Prochaska, 1983) examined how hundreds of clinical psychologists, the plurality (31%) of whom were eclectic, selected their theoretical orientations. Of a list of 14 possible influences on this selection process, outcome research ranked a disappointing tenth. The average rating fell between 'weak influence' and 'some influence'. Our hope for a future replication study is that, as a result of the emerging empirical base in psychotherapy, the influence of outcome research will rank much higher.

(6) The long view. Sibling rivalry among theoretical orientations has a long and undistinguished history in psychotherapy, dating back to Freud. In the infancy of the field, therapy systems, like battling siblings, competed for attention and affection in a 'dogma eat dogma' environment (Larson, 1980). Mutual antipathy and exchange of insults between adherents of rival persuasions were very much the order of the day.

These conflicts are probably a necessary developmental stage to mature synthesis. Kuhn (1970) has described this period as a pre-paradigmatic crisis. Feyerabend (1970), another philosopher of science, has concluded that the interplay between tenacity and proliferation is an essential feature in the actual development of science. The upshot is that the road to sophisticated integration is long, circuitous, and filled with obstacles. An arduous journey is to be expected; steady progress and the long view are to be encouraged.

To use a psychotherapy metaphor, resistance to psychotherapy integration is more chronic and severe than generally recognised. If Kuhn and other philosophers of science are correct in their analyses, most psychotherapists cannot be expected to explore integration naturally or easily. Casual support alone is inadequate to disrupt the historically ingrained and continuously reinforced 'my system, the right system, the only system' attitude which pervades psychotherapy.

In concluding, let us share a quote from Arthur Houts (from Norcross and Thomas, 1988): 'We need to wait for whatever it is that will follow the post-modern era. We are in the post-modern era, but we do not yet know what comes next. There is an old Middle Eastern proverb that applies: "He who plants dates does not live to eat dates". We need to be careful to plant dates rather than pumpkins.'

While eclecticism and integration in psychotherapy have experienced, and will continue to experience, meaningful progress in our lifetimes, the greater legacy of the integrative movement may lie in the future. This legacy, for us, entails the promotion of open inquiry, informed pluralism, empirical research, and intellectual relativism. As with the clinical enterprise itself, the seeds we sow now may produce enticing flowers quickly, but may not bear the sustaining fruit for years to come. Our fervent hope is that we all work diligently enough and live long enough to partake of that fruit together.

Notes

[1] *Membership applications for SEPI may be obtained from Dr George Stricker, Derner Institute of Advanced Psychological Studies, Adelphi University, Garden City, NY 11530, USA. For information on IAEP membership and branches, contact Dr Jusuf Hariman, 6 New Haven Place, St Ives, NSW 2075, Australia.*

[2] *Correspondence regarding JIEP subscriptions and back issues should be addressed to Subscription Department, Brunner/Mazel, 19 Union Square West, New York, NY 10013, USA.*

References

Adams, H.E.: 'The Pernicious Effects of Theoretical Orientations in Clinical Psychology'. *The Clinical Psychologist,* Volume 37, 1984, pp. 90-93.

Allport, G.W.: 'The Fruits of Eclecticism: Bitter or Sweet?' In Allport, G.W. (ed.): *The Person in Psychology.* Boston: Beacon, 1968.

Arkowitz, H.: 'The Role of Theory in Psychotherapy Integration'. *Journal of Integrative and Eclectic Psychotherapy,* Volume 8 No. 1, 1989.

Arkowitz, H., and Messer, S.B. (eds.): *Psychoanalytic and Behavior Therapy: Is Integration Possible?* New York: Plenum, 1984.

Beitman, B.D.: 'Commentary: The Teenage Prosecutor as an Example of Systematic Eclecticism'. In Norcross, J.C. (ed.): *Casebook of Eclectic Psychotherapy.* New York: Brunner/Mazel, 1987.

Beitman, B.D., Chiles, J., and Carlin, A.: 'The Pharmacotherapy- Psychotherapy Triangle: Psychiatrist, Nonmedical Psychotherapist, and Patient'. *Journal of Clinical Psychiatry,* Volume 45, 1984, pp. 458-459.

Beitman, B.D., Goldfried, M.R., and Norcross, J.C.: 'The Movement toward Integrating the Psychotherapies: an Overview'. *American Journal of Psychiatry,* Volume 146, 1989, pp.138-147.

Bergin, A.E.: 'Comment on *Converging Themes in Psychotherapy'.* New York: Springer, 1982.

Bergin, A.E., and Lambert, M.J.: 'The Evaluation of Therapeutic Outcomes'. In Garfield, S.L., and Bergin, A.E. (eds.): *Handbook of Psychotherapy and Behavior Change* (2nd edition). New York: Wiley, 1978.

Beutler, L.E.: *Eclectic Psychotherapy: a Systematic Approach.* New York: Pergamon, 1983.

Beutler, L.E.: 'Systematic Eclectic Psychotherapy'. In Norcross, J.C. (ed.): *Handbook of Eclectic Psychotherapy.* New York: Brunner/Mazel, 1986.

Beutler, L.E., and Clarkin, J.: *Differential Treatment Assignment: Toward Prescriptive Psychological Treatments.* New York: Brunner/Mazel, 1989.

Beutler, L.E., Mahoney, M.J., Norcross, J.C., Prochaska, J.O., Sollod, R.M., and Robertson, M.: 'Training Integrative/Eclectic Psychotherapists II'. *Journal of Integrative and Eclectic Psychotherapy,* Volume 6, 1987, pp. 296-332.

Brabeck, M.M., and Welfel, E.R.: 'Counseling Theory: Understanding the Trend toward Eclecticism from a Developmental Perspective'. *Journal of Counseling and Development,* Volume 63, 1985, pp. 343-349.

Brown, B.S.: 'The Impact of Political and Economic Changes upon Mental Health'. *American Journal of Orthopsychiatry,* Volume 53, 1983, pp. 583-592.

Cross, D.G., and Sheehan, P.W.: 'Classification of Variables in Psychotherapy Research: Therapeutic Change and the Concept of Artifact'. *Psychotherapy: Theory, Research, and Practice,* Volume 18, 1981, pp. 345-355.

Driscoll, R.: 'Ordinary Language as a Common Language for Psychotherapy'. *Journal of Integrative and Eclectic Psychotherapy,* Volume 6, 1987, pp. 184-194.

Dryden, W.: 'Issues in the Eclectic Practice of Individual Therapy'. In Dryden, W. (ed.): *Individual Therapy in Britain.* London: Harper & Row, 1984.

Dryden, W.: 'Eclectic Psychotherapies: a Critique of Leading Approaches'. In Norcross, J.C. (ed.): *Handbook of Eclectic Psychotherapy.* New York: Brunner/Mazel, 1986.

Eysenck, H.J.: 'A Mish-Mash of Theories'. *International Journal of Psychiatry,* Volume 9, 1970, pp. 140-146.

Fensterheim, H.: 'Introduction to Behavioral Psychotherapy'. In Fensterheim, H., and Glazer, H.I. (eds.): *Behavioral Psychotherapy: Basic Principles and Case Studies.* New York: Brunner/Mazel, 1983.

Feyerabend, H.: 'Consolations for the Specialist'. In Lakatos, I., and Musgrave, A.E. (eds.): *Criticism and the Growth of Knowledge.* Cambridge: Cambridge University Press, 1970.

Fischer, J.: 'Eclectic Casework'. In Norcross, J.C. (ed.): *Handbook of Eclectic Psychotherapy.* New York: Brunner/Mazel, 1986.

Fishman, D.B., and Neigher, W.D.: 'American Psychology in the Eighties: Who Will Buy?' *American Psychologist,* Volume 37, 1982, pp. 533-546.

Frances, A.: 'Sigmund Freud: The First Integrative Therapist'. Invited address to the Fourth Annual Convention of the Society for the Exploration of Psychotherapy Integration, Boston, Mass., May 1988.

Frances, A., Clarkin, J., and Perry, S.: *Differential Therapeutics in Psychiatry.* New York: Brunner/Mazel, 1984.

Frank, J.D.: *Persuasion and Healing* (2nd edition). Baltimore: John Hopkins University Press, 1973.

Frank, J.D.: 'The Present Status of Outcome Studies'. *Journal of Consulting and Clinical Psychology*, Volume 47, 1979, pp. 310-316.

Frank, J.D.: 'Therapeutic Components Shared by All Psychotherapies'. In Harvey, J.H., and Parks, M.M. (eds.): *Psychotherapy Research and Behavior Change: 1981 Master Lecture Series*. Washington, DC: American Psychological Association, 1982.

French, T.M.: 'Interrelations between Psychoanalysis and the Experimental Work of Pavlov'. *American Journal of Psychiatry*, Volume 89, 1933, pp. 1165-1203.

Friedling, C., Goldfried, M.R., and Stricker, G.: *Convergence in Psychodynamic and Behavior Therapy*. Paper presented at the annual convention of the Eastern Psychological Association, Baltimore, Maryland, April 1984.

Garfield, S.L.: *Psychotherapy: an Eclectic Approach*. New York: Wiley, 1980.

Garfield, S.L., and Kurtz, R.: 'A Survey of Clinical Psychologists: Characteristics, Activities, and Orientations'. *The Clinical Psychologist,* Volume 28, 1974, pp. 7-10.

Garfield, S.L., and Kurtz, R.: 'A Study of Eclectic Views'. *Journal of Clinical and Consulting Psychology,* Volume 45, 1977, pp. 78-83.

Goldfried, M.R.: 'Toward the Delineation of Therapeutic Change Principles'. *American Psychologist,* Volume 35, 1980, pp. 991-999.

Goldfried, M.R.: 'On the History of Therapeutic Integration'. *Behavior Therapy*, Volume 13, 1982, pp. 572-593.

Goldfried, M.R., and Newman, C.: 'Psychotherapy Integration: an Historical Perspective'. In Norcross, J.C. (ed.): *Handbook of Eclectic Psychotherapy*. New York: Brunner/Mazel, 1986.

Goldfried, M.R., and Padawer, W.: 'Current Status and Future Directions in Psychotherapy'. In Goldfried, M.R. (ed.): *Converging Themes in Psychotherapy: Trends in Psychodynamic, Humanistic, and Behavioral Practice*. New York: Springer, 1982.

Goldfried, M.R., and Safran, J.D.: 'Future Directions in Psychotherapy Integration'. In Norcross, J.C. (ed.): *Handbook of Eclectic Psychotherapy*. New York: Brunner/Mazel, 1986.

Goldstein, A.P., and Stein, N.: *Prescriptive Psychotherapies*. New York: Pergamon, 1976.

Haaga, D.A.: 'A Review of the Common Principles Approach to Integration of Psychotherapies'. *Cognitive Therapy and Research,* Volume 10, 1986, pp.527-538.

Halgin, R.P. (ed.): 'Special Section: Issues in the Supervision of Integrative Psychotherapy'. *Journal of Integrative and Eclectic Psychotherapy,* Volume 7, 1988, pp. 152-180.

Harper, R.A.: *Psychoanalysis and Psychotherapy: 36 Systems.* Englewood Cliffs, NJ: Prentice-Hall, 1959.

Henle, M.: 'Some Problems of Eclecticism'. In *1879 and All That: Essays in the Theory and History of Psychology.* New York: Columbia University Press, 1986.

Jayaratne, S.: 'Characteristics and Theoretical Orientations of Clinical Social Workers: a National Survey'. *Journal of Social Service Research,* Volume 20, 1982, pp. 476-485.

Karasu, T.B.: 'Psychotherapies: an Overview'. *American Journal of Psychiatry,* Volume 134, 1977, pp. 851-863.

Karasu, T.B.: 'The Specificity versus Nonspecificity Dilemma: Toward Identifying Therapeutic Change Agents'. *American Journal of Psychiatry,* Volume 143, 1986, pp. 687-695.

Kiesler, D.J.: 'Some Myths of Psychotherapy Research and the Search for a Paradigm'. *Psychological Bulletin,* Volume 65, 1966, pp. 110-136.

Kuhn, T.S.: *The Structure of Scientific Revolutions* (2nd edition). Chicago: University of Chicago Press, 1970.

Lambert, M.J.: 'Implications of Psychotherapy Outcome Research for Eclectic Psychotherapy'. In Norcross, J.C. (ed.): *Handbook of Eclectic Psychotherapy.* New York: Brunner/Mazel, 1986.

Landsman, J.T., and Dawes, R.M.: 'Smith and Glass' Conclusions Stand Up Under Scrutiny'. *American Psychologist,* Volume 37, 1982, pp. 504-516.

Landsman, J.T.: ' Not an Adversity but a Welcome Diversity.' Paper presented at the meeting of the American Psychological Association, New Orleans, August 1974.

Larson, D.: 'Therapeutic Schools, Styles, and Schoolism: a National Survey'. *Journal of Humanistic Psychology,* Volume 20, 1980,pp. 3-20.

Lazarus, A.A.: 'In Support of Technical Eclecticism'. *Psychological Reports,* Volume 21, 1967, pp. 415-416.

Lazarus, A.A.: *Multimodal Behavior Therapy.* New York: Springer, 1976.

Lazarus, A.A.: 'Has Behavior Therapy Outlived its Usefulness?' *American Psychologist,* Volume 32, 1977, pp. 550-554.

Lazarus, A.A.: *The Practice of Multimodal Therapy.* New York: McGraw-Hill, 1981.

Lazarus, A.A.: 'Multimodal Therapy'. In Corsini, R.J. (ed.): *Current Psychotherapies* (3rd edition). Itasca, Illinois: Peacock, 1984.

Lazarus, A.A. (ed.): *Casebook of Multimodal Therapy.* New York: Guilford, 1985.

Lazarus, A.A.: 'From the Ashes'. *International Journal of Eclectic Psychotherapy,* Volume 5, 1986, pp. 241-242.

London, P.: 'Ecumenism in Psychotherapy'. *Contemporary Psychology,* Volume 28, 1983, pp. 507-508.

London, P.:'Metamorphosis in Psychotherapy: Slouching toward Integration'. *Journal of Integrative and Eclectic Psychotherapy,* Volume 7, 1988, pp. 3-12.

Luborsky, L., Singer, B., and Luborsky, L.: 'Comparative Studies of Psychotherapies: Is it True that "Everybody has Won and All Must Have Prizes?"'. *Archives of General Psychiatry,* Volume 32, 1975, pp. 995-1008.

Lunde, D.T.: 'Eclectic and Integrated Theory: Gordon Allport and Others'. In Burton, A. (ed.): *Operational Theories of Personality.* New York: Brunner/Mazel, 1974.

Mahoney, M.J., Norcross, J.C., Prochaska, J.O., and Missar, C.D.: 'Psychological Development and Optimal Psychotherapy: Converging Perspectives among Clinical Psychologists'. *Journal of Integrative and Eclectic Psychotherapy,* Volume 8, 1989.

Marmor, J.: 'Recent Trends in Psychotherapy'. *American Journal of Psychiatry,* Volume 137, 1980, pp. 409-416.

Messer, S.B.: 'Integrating Psychoanalytic and Behaviour Therapy: Limitations, Possibilities and Trade-Offs'. *British Journal of Clinical Psychology,* Volume 22, 1983, pp. 131-132.

Messer, S.B.: ' Eclecticism in Psychotherapy: Underlying Assumptions, Problems, and Trade-Offs'. In Norcross, J.C. (ed.): *Handbook of Eclectic Psychotherapy.* New York: Brunner/Mazel, 1986(a).

Messer, S.B.: 'Behavioral and Psychoanalytic Perspectives at Therapeutic Choice Points'. *American Psychologist,* Volume 41, 1986(b), pp. 1261-1272.

Messer, S.B.: 'Can the Tower of Babel be Completed? A Critique of the Common Language Proposal'. *Journal of Integrative and Eclectic Psychotherapy*, Volume 6, 1987, pp. 195-199.

Messer, S.B., and Winokur, M.: 'Some Limits to the Integration of Psychoanalytic and Behavior Therapy'. *American Psychologist*, Volume 35, 1980, pp. 818-827.

Messer, S.B., and Winokur, M.: 'Ways of Knowing and Visions of Reality in Psychoanalytic Therapy and Behavior Therapy'. In Arkowitz, H., and Messer, S.B. (eds.): *Psychoanalytic Therapy and Behavior Therapy: Is Integration Possible?* New York: Plenum, 1984.

Miller, M.H.: 'We are Good - They are Bad'. *Journal of Nervous and Mental Disease*, Volume 173, 1985, pp. 279-281.

Moultrup, D.: 'Integration: a Coming of Age'. *Contemporary Family Therapy*, Volume 8, 1986, pp. 157-167.

Norcross, J.C.: 'All in the Family? On Therapeutic Commonalities'. *American Psychologist*, Volume 36, 1981, pp. 1544- 1545.

Norcross, J.C.: 'For Discriminating Clinicians Only'. *Contemporary Psychology*, Volume 30, 1985, pp. 757-758.

Norcross, J.C. (ed.): *Handbook of Eclectic Psychotherapy*. New York: Brunner/Mazel, 1986.

Norcross, J.C. (ed.): 'Special Section: Toward a Common Language for Psychotherapy'. *Journal of Integrative and Eclectic Psychotherapy*, Volume 4, 1987, pp. 165-205.

Norcross, J.C.: 'The Exclusivity Myth and Equifinality Principle in Psychotherapy'. *Journal of Integrative and Eclectic Psychotherapy*, Volume 7, 1988, pp. 415-421.

Norcross, J.C., and Napolitano, G.: 'Defining our Journal and Ourselves'. *International Journal of Eclectic Psychotherapy*, Volume 5, 1986, pp. 249-255.

Norcross, J.C., and Prochaska, J.O.: ' Clinicians' Theoretical Orientations: Selection, Utilization, and Efficacy'. *Professional Psychology*, Volume 14, 1983, pp. 197-208.

Norcross, J.C., and Prochaska, J.O.: 'A Study of Eclectic (and Integrative) Views Revisited'. *Professional Psychology: Research and Practice*, Volume 19, 1988, pp. 170-174.

Norcross, J.C., and Thomas, B.L.: 'What's Stopping Us Now? Obstacles to Psychotherapy Integration'. *Journal of Integrative and Eclectic Psychotherapy*, Volume 7, 1988, pp.74-80.

Norcross, J.C., Beutler, L.E., Clarkin, J.F., DiClemente, C.C., Halgin, R.P., Frances, A., Prochaska, J.O., Robertson, M., and Suedfeld, P.: 'Training Integrative/Eclectic Psychotherapists'. *International Journal of Eclectic Psychotherapy*, Volume 5, 1986, pp. 71-94.

Norcross, J.C., Prochaska, J.O.,and Gallagher, K.M.: 'Clinical Psychologists in the 1980's: I. Demographics, Affiliations, and Satisfactions'. *The Clinical Psychologist*, Volume 42 No. 2, 1989.

Omer, H., and London, P.: 'Metamorphosis in Psychotherapy: End of the Systems Era'. *Psychotherapy*, Volume 25, 1988, pp. 171-180.

Parloff, M.B.: 'Shopping for the Right Therapy'. *Saturday Review*, 21 February 1976, pp. 135- 142.

Parloff, M.B.: 'Can Psychotherapy Research Guide the Policymaker?: a Little Knowledge May Be a Dangerous Thing'. *American Psychologist*, Volume 34, 1979, pp. 296-306.

Paul, G.L.: 'Strategy of Outcome Research in Psychotherapy'. *Journal of Consulting Psychology*, Volume 31, 1987, pp. 109-119.

Perlman, B.: 'A National Survey of APA Affiliated Master-Level Clinicians: Description and Comparison'. *Professional Psychology: Research and Practice*, Volume 16, 1985, pp. 553-564.

Peterson, D.R., Eaton, M.M., Levine, A.R., and Snepp, F.P.: 'Career Experiences of Doctors of Psychology'. *Professional Psychology*, Volume 13, 1982, pp. 268-277.

Pinsof, W.M.: 'Integrative Problem-Centered Therapy: Toward the Synthesis of Family and Individual Psychotherapies'. *Journal of Marital and Family Therapy*, Volume 9, 1983, pp. 19-35.

Prochaska, J.O.: *Systems of Psychotherapy: a Transtheoretical Analysis* (2nd edition). Homewood, Illinois: Dorsey, 1984.

Prochaska, J.O., and DiClemente, C.C.: *The Transtheoretical Approach: Crossing the Traditional Boundaries of Therapy*. Homewood, Illinois: Dow Jones-Irwin, 1984.

Prochaska, J.O., and Norcross, J.C.: 'The Future of Psychotherapy: a Delphi Poll'. *Professional Psychology*, Volume 13, 1982, pp. 620-627.

Prochaska, J.O., and Norcross, J.C.: 'Contemporary Psychotherapists: a National Survey of Characteristics, Practices, Orientations, and Attitudes'. *Psychotherapy: Theory, Research and Practice,* Volume 20, 1983, pp. 161-173.

Robertson, M.: 'Some Observations from an Eclectic Therapist'. *Psychotherapy: Theory, Research, and Practice*, Volume 16, 1979, pp. 18-21.

Robertson, M.: 'Training Eclectic Psychotherapists'. In Norcross, J.C. (ed.): *Handbook of Eclectic Psychotherapy.* New York: Brunner/Mazel, 1986.

Rotter, J.B.: *Social Learning and Clinical Psychology.* Englewood Cliffs, NJ: Prentice-Hall, 1954.

Ryle, A.: 'Cognitive Psychology as a Common Language for Psychotherapy'. *Journal of Integrative and Eclectic Psychotherapy.* Volume 6, 1987, pp. 168-172.

Smith, D.S.: 'Trends in Counseling and Psychotherapy'. *American Psychologist,* Volume 37, 1982, pp. 802- 809.

Smith, M.L., Glass, G.V., and Miller, T.J.: *The Benefits of Psychotherapy.* Baltimore: John Hopkins University Press, 1980.

Stiles, W.B., Shapiro, S.A., and Elliot, R.: 'Are All Psychotherapies Equivalent?' *American Psychologist,* Volume 41, 1986, pp. 165-180.

Stricker, G.: 'Some Viable Suggestions for Integrating Psychotherapies'. Paper presented at the second annual conference of the Society for the Exploration of Psychotherapy Integration, Toronto, May 1986.

Strong, S.R.: 'Interpersonal Theory as a Common Language for Psychotherapy'. *Journal of Integrative and Eclectic Psychotherapy*, Volume 6, 1987, pp. 173-183.

Strupp, H.H.: 'On the Basic Ingredients of Psychotherapy'. *Journal of Clinical and Consulting Psychology,* Volume 41, 1973, pp. 1-8.

Strupp, H.H.: 'The Outcome Problem in Psychotherapy: Contemporary Perspectives'. In Harvey, J.H., and Parks, M.M. (eds.): *Psychotherapy Research and Behavior Change: 1981 Master Lecture Series.* Washington, DC: American Psychological Association, 1982.

Wachtel, P.L.: *Psychoanalysis and Behavior Therapy: Toward an Integration.* New York: Basic Books, 1977.

Wachtel, P.L.: 'Integration Misunderstood'. *British Journal of Clinical Psychology*, Volume 22, 1983, pp. 129-130.

ECLECTICISM AND INTEGRATION

Wachtel, P.L.: *Action and Insight.* New York: Guilford, 1987. Watkins, C.E., Lopez, F.G., Campbell, V.L., and Himmell, C.D.: 'Contemporary Counseling Psychology: Results of a National Survey'. *Journal of Counseling Psychology,* Volume 33, 1986, pp. 301-309.

Weiner, I.B.: *Principles of Psychotherapy.* New York: Wiley, 1975.

Wilson, G.T.: 'Psychotherapy Process and Procedure: the Behavioral Mandate'. *Behavior Therapy,* Volume 12, 1982, pp. 291- 312.

Wolfe, B.E., and Goldfried., M.R.: 'Research on Psychotherapy Integration: Recommendations and Conclusions from an NIMH Workshop'. *Journal of Consulting and Clinical Psychology,* Volume 56, 1988, pp. 448-451.

Yates, A.J.: 'Behaviour Therapy and Psychodynamic Therapy: Basic Conflict or Reconciliation and Integration?' *British Journal of Clinical Psychology,* Volume 22, 1983, pp. 107-125.

This article is based in part on an invited plenary address to the First International Conference on Eclectic Psychotherapy, San Miguel de Allende, Mexico, December 1988.

CHAPTER 2

Why I am an Eclectic (Not an Integrationist)

Arnold A. Lazarus

Graduate School of Applied and Professional Psychology

Rutgers State University of New Jersey, USA

Eclecticism is a complex set of structures and conceptions. Unsystematic eclecticism and integrationism are based mainly upon personal preference and subjective judgement, whereas systematic, prescriptive (technical) eclecticism is guided by the impact of patient qualities, clinical skills, and specific techniques. Fusionists arbitrarily blend what they consider helpful ingredients from two seemingly disparate orientations and end up in theoretical and clinical dead ends. Eventually, a unified theory is called for, together with a superordinate structure that will reconcile divergent points of view (integrationism). Nevertheless, our current pre-paradigmatic level of understanding precludes such a synthesis at present. To pretend otherwise only breeds confusion worse confounded. Meanwhile, a problem-focused approach to therapy is recommended, one that eschews general labels and tries to reach consensus on the specification of goals, problems, strategies, and systematic measurements (technical eclecticism). Integrationists seem to have overlooked the false conclusions of meta-analysis and contend that all treatment outcomes are similar. We are now in a position to recommend specific treatments for specific problems. To ignore technique specificity is a serious breach of professional responsibility.

Overview

Definitional and descriptive grounds may determine whether one favours eclecticism over integrationism, or *vice versa*. Beitman (in a previous draft of chapter 3) claimed that eclectics merely gather bits of data, eschew general principles, advocate a conceptually limited stance, provide no model for therapeutic change processes, ignore the individual personality of the therapist, emphasise strict adherence to prescribed therapist behaviours in place of clinical flexibility, and in the final analysis, only administer simple or complex rote techniques. If any of these assertions were true, I would be a vociferous opponent of eclecticism.

The first point to be underscored is that eclecticism is not a single edifice or a unitary construct (Lazarus, 1988). Some eclectics wish to achieve a synthesis of seemingly divergent approaches; others may aspire to find synergistic combinations of various principles and procedures. Norcross (1986) has shown that eclecticism is a complex set of structures and conceptions, comprising, among others, a transtheoretical stance, an atheoretical position, a synthetic integration, a structural-phenomenological approach, and one that is governed by a preferred theory but also borrows techniques from other orientations (*technical eclecticism*). Nevertheless, there is still a widespread and persistent tendency to regard 'eclecticism' as a single entity. Thus, Eysenck (1986, p. 378) stated that 'an eclectic point of view by definition means an anti-scientific point of view: eclecticism has always been the enemy of scientific understanding'. This misguided conclusion stems from the refusal to recognise that convergence, rapprochement, and data-based eclecticism can rest on the bedrock of rigorous scientific inquiry.

Haphazard, idiosyncratic eclecticism wherein clinicians and theorists incorporate various ideas and methods on the basis of subjective appeal, should not be bracketed with systematic eclecticism which is based on years of painstaking research and clinical work (Lazarus, 1988). Unsystematic eclecticism is practised by therapists who require neither a coherent rationale nor empirical validation for the methods they employ. Beitman contends that the form of integration selected, plus the strategies and tactics embraced, are largely determined by the individual personality of the therapist. But systematic prescriptive (technical) eclectics do not simply choose 'whatever feels right'. They base their endeavours on data from the threefold impact of patient qualities, clinical skills, and specific techniques (Lazarus, 1987).

It may be helpful to distinguish between *eclecticism* and *fusionism* (Lazarus, 1988). Fusionists tend to blend what they regard as the most helpful notions and ingredients from two seemingly disparate orientations. Starting with a paper by French (1933), the proposed fusion that has received the greatest attention is the attempted consolidation of behaviour therapy and psychoanalysis (e.g. Arkowitz and Messer, 1984; Goldfried, 1982; Marmor and Woods, 1980; Wachtel, 1977). More recent fusionists propose to integrate cognitive-behaviour therapy and Gestalt therapy (Fodor, 1987), and systems and psychodynamic methods (Kirschner and Kirschner, 1986). Any bimodal melding strikes me as arbitrary and capricious. If this trend proliferates, we can anticipate any number of strange bedfellows - Adlerian/Morita; Jungian/Rational-Emotive; Primal/Existential (the list is almost endless).

When a therapist identifies his or her orientation as 'eclectic', this conveys nothing of meaning or substance. Differences among various eclectics may surpass even rigid school adherents. The entire field of psychotherapy, I believe, needs to drop generic labels - eclectic, psychodynamic, behavioural, humanistic, etc. - to be replaced by consensus on the specification of goals and problems, the specification of strategies to achieve these goals and remedy these problems, and the systematic measurement of the relative success of these different techniques and processes (Lazarus, 1989). If and when the foregoing have been achieved, we will be in a position to move toward integration. At this stage of our development, integrationism seems to me premature and strongly ill-advised.

My main objections to integrationism

In their attempt to avoid ideological rigidity, integrationists try to meld disparate ideas and conflicting schools into a co-operative and harmonious whole. While the field of psychotherapy is in need of a unified theory, a superordinate umbrella that will reconcile divergent points of emphasis and blend multiple concepts and techniques into a coherent framework, the pre-paradigmatic level at which we presently function is far from this ideal. Meanwhile, to my way of thinking, it is a mistake to blend seemingly compatible theories from different schools in the hope of harnessing greater energy from each. The main problem here is that, upon close scrutiny, what seems to be interchangeable among different theories, often turns out to be totally irreconcilable. As Messer and Winokur (1981) have shown, 'in many instances what appears at first glance as commonality becomes, on closer inspection, so basic a difference that we wonder on what grounds therapists of different theoretical persuasions can meet' (p. 1547). In their search for common components, integrationists are apt to emphasise insignificant similarities and gloss over significant differences.

Hence my emphasis on *technical eclecticism* (e.g. Lazarus, 1967; 1971; 1987; 1989), which looks mainly to social and cognitive learning theory (Bandura, 1986) for explanatory constructs, since its tenets are grounded in research and are open to verification and disproof. By operating from a consistent, testable, theoretical base and then drawing on useful techniques from any discipline without necessarily subscribing to the theoretical underpinnings that gave rise to the techniques in question, one avoids the jumble, the *melange*, and the subjective bias of theoretical eclecticism or integrationism. As London (1964) observed: 'However interesting, plausible, and appealing a theory may be, it is techniques, not theories, that are actually used on people. Study of the effects of psychotherapy, therefore, is always the study of the effectiveness of techniques' (p.33). Technical eclectics regard the therapeutic relationship as the soil that enables the techniques to take root (Lazarus and Fay, 1984).

37

It is most important to bear in mind that one remains theoretically consistent when practising technical eclecticism (cf. Dryden, 1987). Moreover, while techniques are strongly emphasised, this is not to the detriment of a conceptual and theoretical appreciation of the issues at stake. Technical eclecticism, as many have erroneously assumed, is not anti-theoretical or atheoretical. Unfortunately, some who call themselves technical eclectics have tended to select methods and styles that *they* individually consider appropriate, based on guiding principles that are at best questionable.

Thus, although I see technical eclecticism as an evolutionary step towards eventual integrationism, I maintain that it is extremely premature to embark on 'the conceptual synthesis of diverse theoretical systems' (Beitman *et al.*, 1989, p. 139). I fear that many of our current theories will suffer the same fate as Gall and Spurzheim's studies on phrenology. Their work on physiognomy and craniology was based on the most advanced neurology, physiology and psychology of their day, and their theories of personality were acclaimed by scientists, scholars, and professionals in France, Germany, Switzerland, Scotland, England, Ireland, and America. In 1823, *The British Phrenological Journal* was launched, and in 1838, the New York Institute of Phrenology founded *The American Phrenological Journal* which finally ceased publication in 1911 after its 124th volume. The theory and practice of phrenology enjoyed its greatest popularity in the 1850s. Today it is but a roost for charlatans.

Similarly, I predict that most of Freud's ideas about the unconscious will fall into total disrepute. So when integrationists start borrowing and blending psychoanalytic tenets with behavioural constructs, to which they may add ingredients from any number of additional systems, it seems to me that they emerge with a confused and confusing farrago, thus taking the field aeons away from the coherent super-organising theory to which they aspire. And in place of the superstructure under whose umbrella theoretical differences can be subsumed and reconciled, we will be handed nothing but syncretistic muddles.

Is technical eclecticism merely a collection of techniques?

Let it be understood that I am in favour of striving toward eventual integration-ism. The fragmented, disparate methods and theories that presently charac-terise our field need to be replaced by a coherent, unified, and consolidated body of knowledge. But, as already mentioned, I believe that premature inte-grationism will only defeat these ends. Can technical eclecticism point the way?

For me, the seeds of technical eclecticism were sown in 1964 at the Veter-ans Administration Hospital in Palo Alto, California, where I had treated three patients behind a one-way mirror for approximately three months. The audi-ence comprised a wide array of professionals and graduate students from the Bay area who were interested in seeing the new methods and techniques of be-haviour therapy in action. It was the heyday of my behaviouristic zeal, and I demonstrated the use of systematic desensitisation based on relaxation, asser-tiveness training, homework assignments (especially graded *in vivo* excursions), stimulus control, and various ancillary procedures. All three patients had proved unresponsive to traditional psychotherapy. One of them was bulimic and the excessive bingeing and purging presented a problem of considerable clinical urgency. My use of 'behaviour therapy' resulted in a dramatic remission within three months - the patient was eating normally, gained much-needed weight, and was discharged from the hospital. Improvement in the other two patients, though less dramatic, was also quite apparent. My colleagues who had observed the entire course of treatment were asked whether they could specify the processes to which the therapeutic benefits might be ascribed.

No agreement could be reached concerning the reasons for the undis-puted gains. My own views at that time leaned heavily upon notions of counter-conditioning and extinction. The views of my colleagues, however, were as different from my own as they were from one another's. Rich varieties of the-oretical opinions were offered and sometimes generated heated arguments. It was obvious that the many (often divergent) theoretical positions could not all be correct. But it was possible that every theoretical explanation, including my own, could be false. Thus, I became convinced of the futility of *post hoc* theorising, and felt that genuine progress would ensue if therapists were willing and able to spell out precisely what operations they perform with various patients. It then seemed logical to assume that all therapies may succeed, in so far as they do, for reasons other than the causal factors specified in their theories. This paved the way to accept all empirically valid techniques without having to subscribe to their underlying theories, and a brief statement on technical eclecticism (Lazarus, 1967) was offered and subsequently elaborated (e.g. Lazarus, 1971; 1987; 1989).

It is important to underscore that technical eclecticism is not merely a collection of techniques but operates within a consistent theoretical base, and endeavours to pinpoint various processes and principles. For example, one may start with Pavlovian conditioning and inquire whether 'associations and relations among events' (Rescorla, 1988) adequately explain the factors that shape and maintain human behaviour. In accounting for the variance, it will soon be necessary to add additional concepts such as 'modelling and imitation', 'nonconscious processes', 'defensive reactions', 'idiosyncratic perceptions', 'metacommunications', and 'physiological thresholds' (nonconscious processes should not be confused with the reified unconscious mind, and defensive reactions are not synonymous with the mechanisms of defence - see Lazarus, 1989).

The point at issue is that a technically eclectic stance endeavours to use effective techniques from any persuasion, while also searching for guiding principles and concepts, and tries to avoid the needless addition or multiplication of explanatory principles. Unfortunately, most therapists are guided by selective perception and personal preference. The hallmark of technical eclecticism is the use of prescriptive treatments based on empirical evidence and client need, rather than theoretical and personal predisposition (cf. Beitman *et al.*, 1989; Frances *et al.*, 1984; Karasu, 1989). As Norcross (1986, p. 11) has noted: 'the promise of eclecticism is the development of a comprehensive psychotherapy based on a unified and empirical body of work'. I concur and would point out that if technical eclecticism amounted to no more than a grab-bag of techniques, this objective would never be achieved.

Additional problems with integrationism

It is unfortunate that 'when instructed to select the type of integration that they practice, the majority of eclectics - 61% and 65% - chose theoretical integration' (Norcross and Grencavage, chapter 1). There is a seductive quality to the notion of being able to select the best elements from the different schools of therapy. As I have tried to emphasise, counsellors who mingle techniques, while mixing theories and formats across various schools of thought, merely breed confusion worse confounded. But integrationism (as opposed to eclecticism) seems to fall into several other traps.

Semantic baggage and ill-defined labels. My form of technical eclecticism avoids vague terms and labels and strives for operational and quantifiable descriptions. For example, terms like 'avoidance behaviour', 'tachycardia' and 'negative self-statements' are preferred to 'neurosis' or even 'anxiety'. A *problem-focused approach* to therapy is favoured, one that expedites clinical decision-making and sidesteps the quagmire of putative complexes and other untestable intrapsychic entities. In the field of organic medicine, Weed (1968) was among the first to underscore the advantages of developing a problem-oriented record approach in place of the usual diagnostic labels. This emphasis upon problem specification was introduced into psychiatry by Hayes-Roth *et al.* (1972).

But integrationists, even when discussing strategies, tend to converse at a level of meaningless abstraction. I refer you to table 2 in Norcross and Grencavage's chapter. One integrationist may state: 'I select my tactics from an interpersonal and humanistic perspective.' Another might say: 'I use a combination of systems and behavioural strategies.' It is my contention that these labels convey no clear meanings whatsoever. Some 'humanists' are very 'behavioural'. Some 'systems' theorists are 'cognitive', wheras others are 'psychoanalytic', or 'interpersonal'. Continued use of nebulous labels seriously hinders our efforts to achieve open inquiry, informed pluralism, and intellectual relativism. In the final analysis, unless therapists stop hiding behind labels and are able and willing to state precisely what they do, and don't do, to and with their clients at specific choice points (Lazarus and Messer, 1988), psychotherapy will continue to be guided by faith rather than fact.

The equality-of-outcomes myth. One of the spearheads of integrationism is the 'everybody has won' conclusion (Luborsky *et al.*, 1975) which asserts that all psychotherapies are equally effective and that there are negligible differences among the different treatment methods. The work of Smith *et al.* (1980) on meta-analysis has bolstered this idea, but it has been shown that the conclusions of meta-analysis can be extremely misleading (Kendall, 1987; Wilson, 1982; 1985; Wilson and Rachman, 1983). Wilson (1987) points out that despite numerous flaws and inaccuracies in Smith *et al.*'s (1980) study, its conclusions are widely cited in the literature. In fact, when selecting 'well controlled' studies, Smith *et al.* found behaviour therapy to be significantly superior to psychodynamic and other verbal therapies. Subsequent meta-analyses (e.g. Andrews *et al.*, 1983; Shapiro and Shapiro, 1983) have consistently concluded that behaviour therapy is superior to all other forms of psychological treatment. This is not surprising because the range of techniques employed by present-day cognitive-behavioural therapists suggests that most are technically eclectic (Kendall, 1987). Yet Beitman *et al.* (1989) and Norcross and Grencavage (chapter 1) insist that it has not been shown that one therapeutic approach is superior to another.

There are indeed many mildly or even moderately disturbed individuals who will probably respond equally well to any non-noxious therapy and therapist, and here, the equivalence conclusion will most likely be upheld. It is also probable that minimal outcome differences will emerge in a large sample of unselected patients that included a fair number of pervasively anxious individuals: schizophrenics; substance abusers; sociopathic, anti-social, and borderline personalities; encrusted obsessive-compulsive sufferers; impulse control and dissociative disorders; and various undifferentiated somatoform disorders.

But Beitman *et al.*'s (1989, p. 140) statement that 'with few exceptions, there is little compelling evidence to recommend the use of one form of psychotherapy over another in the treatment of specific problems' flies in the face of the facts. There *are* specific treatments for specific problems and specific

42

strategies for specific syndromes (Kazdin and Wilson, 1978; Lazarus, 1984). For example, the clinical reports on the use of specific techniques for overcoming sexual inadequacy provided by Wolpe and Lazarus (1966) were confirmed and amplified by Masters and Johnson (1970), and further refined by subsequent research (e.g. Leiblum and Pervin, 1980; Leiblum and Rosen, 1988; LoPiccolo and LoPiccolo, 1978). It is almost a quarter of a century since Paul (1966) in treating public-speaking anxieties, showed significantly superior effectiveness for systematic desensitisation compared to insight therapy and an attention-placebo group. With regard to the treatment of phobic disorders, Bandura (1986) cites numerous studies that show various modelling and exposure techniques to be superior to other treatments. But apart from phobias, tics, enuresis, and habit disorders, there are also data pertaining to specific treatments of choice for certain anxiety and depressive disorders, stress-related difficulties, social skill deficits, obsessive-compulsive disorders, pain and other aspects of behavioural medicine (see Barlow, 1988; Hersen and Bellack, 1985; Rachman and Wilson, 1980; Woolfolk and Lehrer, 1984).

In treating agoraphobia, for instance, both flooding and exposure have been shown to be more effective than alternative psychological methods (Chambless, 1985; O'Leary and Wilson, 1987). In the psychological treatment of panic disorders, the methods of choice appear to be exposure combined with cognitive restructuring and respiratory control training (Barlow, 1988; Clark *et al.*, 1985). (Biological psychiatrists tend to favour the use of antidepressant drugs and other psychotropic medications for the treatment of panic, but I am concerned about untoward side-effects, and am unimpressed with the follow-up data once the drugs are discontinued.)

There are many other specific treatment effects that can be mentioned. Blackburn *et al.* (1981) confirmed the finding that cognitive therapy is superior to antidepressant medication for depressed outpatients (Rush *et al.*, 1977). Exposure and response prevention have proved consistently effective in eliminating compulsive rituals (Grayson *et al.*, 1985; Mills *et al.*, 1973). In the treatment of bulimia nervosa, there is much evidence to recommend the specific use of cognitive-behavioural procedures (e.g. Fairburn, 1988; Wilson and Smith, 1987). Additional examples can be cited, but perhaps the foregoing will suffice to challenge the notion that there are only a few instances in which one treatment can be recommended over another for specific problems.

In essence, technical efficacy is likely to suffer when one's attention is focused on the amalgamation of diverse ideologies. One good theory and a panoply of techniques can accomplish much more than the fusion and melding of different theories. In this regard, Beutler (1989) has marshalled cogent arguments against looking for or finding a suitably relevant and accepted integrated theory, and he presents a compelling case in favour of technical eclecticism.

Conclusion

To a large extent, this entire debate is an exercise in sophistry. As mentioned at the beginning of this paper, so much hinges on conceptual, definitional, and semantic issues, that the positions reflected and advocated by Norcross and Grencavage, Beitman, Messer and myself, can be regarded as somewhat specious. In place of conceptual and terminological debates, I have tried to provide a systematic, comprehensive psychotherapeutic structure that pragmatically combines techniques, strategies, and modalities and addresses specific assessment and treatment operations. I have called this approach 'multimodal therapy' (Lazarus, 1976; 1985; 1987; 1989) and offer it as a heuristic for diagnosing and treating discrete and interactive problems within and among each vector of 'personality'. It addresses such factors as 'client readiness' (cf. Howard *et al.*, 1987; Prochaska and DiClemente, 1986), spells out when to treat family systems rather than individuals, and *vice versa*, and emphasises *goodness of fit* in terms of the patient's expectancies, therapist-patient compatibility, and the selection of appropriate techniques. In essence, the multimodal orientation asserts that patients are usually troubled by a multitude of specific problems that should be dealt with by a similar multitude of specific treatments. Each area of a client's BASIC ID is addressed (B = Behaviour, A = Affect, S = Sensation, I = Imagery, C = Cognition, I = Interpersonal relationships, D = Drugs/Biological factors). It matters little whether we label the foregoing 'eclecticism' or 'integrationism'. Perhaps we can all agree that we need more rational and empirical bases in place of purely notional and speculative conceptualisations, and that more clearly operationalised and concretised therapist-decision-making processes need to be articulated. To step out of the field of theology and enter the realm of science, psychotherapy must replace hermeneutic abstractions with testable operations.

CHAPTER 2

References

Andrews, G., Moran, C., and Hall, W.: 'Agoraphobia: a Meta-Analysis of Treatment Outcome Studies'. Unpublished manuscript, University of New South Wales Medical School, Australia, 1983.

Arkowitz, H., and Messer, S.B. (eds.): *Psychoanalytic Therapy and Behavior Therapy: Is Integration Possible?* New York: Plenum, 1984.

Bandura, A.: *Social Foundations of Thought and Action: a Social Cognitive Theory.* Englewood Cliffs, NJ: Prentice-Hall, 1986.

Barlow, D.H.: *Anxiety and its Disorders: the Nature and Treatment of Anxiety and Panic.* New York: Guilford, 1988.

Beitman, B.D., Goldfried, M.R., and Norcross. J.C.: 'The Movement toward Integrating the Psychotherapies: an Overview'. *American Journal of Psychiatry,* Volume 146, 1989, pp. 138- 147.

Beutler, L.E.: 'The Misplaced Role of Theory in Psychotherapy Integration'. *Journal of Integrative and Eclectic Psychotherapy,* 1989 (in press).

Blackburn, I.M., Bishop, S., Glen, A.I.M., Whally, L.J., and Christie, J.E.: 'The Efficacy of Cognitive Therapy in Depression: a Treatment Trial Using Cognitive Therapy and Pharmacotherapy, Each Alone and in Combination'. *British Journal of Psychiatry,* Volume 139, 1981, pp. 181-189.

Chambless, D.L.: 'Agoraphobia'. In Hersen, M., and Bellack, A.S. (eds.): *Handbook of Clinical Behavior Therapy with Adults.* New York: Plenum, 1985.

Clark, D.M., Salkovskis, P.M., and Chalkley, A.J.: 'Respiratory Control as a Treatment for Panic Attacks'. *Journal of Behavior Therapy and Experimental Psychiatry,* Volume 16, 1985, pp.23-30.

Dryden, W.: 'Theoretically Consistent Eclecticism: Humanizing a Computer "Addict"'. In Norcross, J.C. (ed.): *Casebook of Eclectic Psychotherapy.* New York: Brunner/Mazel, 1987.

Eysenck, H.J.: 'Consensus and Controversy: Two Types of Science'. In Modgil, S., and Modgil, C. (eds.): *Hans Eysenck: Consensus and Controversy.* London: Falmer, 1986.

Fairburn, C.G.: 'The Current Status of the Psychological Treatments for Bulimia Nervosa'. *Journal of Psychosomatic Research,* Volume 32, 1988, pp. 635-645.

Fodor, I.G.: 'Moving beyond Cognitive Behavior Therapy: Integrating Gestalt Therapy to Facilitate Personal and Inter-Personal Awareness'. In Jacobson, N.S. (ed.): *Psychotherapists in Clinical Practice*. New York: Guilford, 1987.

Frances, A., Clarkin, J., and Perry, S.: *Differential Therapeutics in Psychiatry*. New York: Brunner/Mazel, 1984.

French, T.M.: 'Interrelations between Psychoanalysis and the Experimental Work of Pavlov'. *American Journal of Psychiatry*, Volume 89, 1933, pp. 1165-1203.

Goldfried, M.R.: *Converging Themes in Psychotherapy*. New York: Springer, 1982.

Grayson, J.B., Foa, E.B., and Steketee, G.: 'Obsessive-Compulsive Disorder'. In Hersen, M., and Bellack, A.S. (eds.): *Handbook of Clinical Behavior Therapy with Adults*. New York: Plenum, 1985.

Hayes-Roth, F., Longabaugh, R., and Ryback, R.: 'The Problem-Oriented Medical Record and Psychiatry'. *British Journal of Psychiatry*, Volume 121, 1972, pp. 27-34.

Hersen, M., and Bellack, A.S. (eds.): *Handbook of Clinical Behavior Therapy with Adults*. New York: Plenum, 1985.

Howard, G.S., Nance, D.W., and Myers, P.: *Adaptive Counseling and Therapy*. San Francisco: Jossey-Bass, 1987.

Karasu, T.B.: 'New Frontiers in Psychotherapy'. *Journal of Clinical Psychiatry*, Volume 50, 1989, pp. 46-52.

Kazdin, A.E., and Wilson, G.T.: *Evaluation of Behavior Therapy: Issues, Evidence and Research Strategies*. Cambridge, Massachusetts: Ballinger, 1978.

Kendall, P.C.: 'Cognitive Processes and Procedures in Behavior Therapy'. In Wilson, G.T., Franks, C.M., Kendall, P.C., and Foreyt, J.P. (eds.): *Review of Behavior Therapy: Theory and Practice*, Volume 11. New York: Guilford, 1987.

Kirschner, D.A., and Kirschner, S.: *Comprehensive Family Therapy: an Integration of Systemic and Psychodynamic Treatment Models*. New York: Brunner/Mazel, 1986.

Lazarus, A.A.: 'In Support of Technical Eclecticism'. *Psychological Reports*, Volume 21, 1967, pp. 415-416.

Lazarus, A.A.: *Behavior Therapy and Beyond*. New York: McGraw-Hill, 1971.

Lazarus, A.A.: *Multimodal Behavior Therapy*. New York: Springer, 1976.

CHAPTER 2

Lazarus, A.A.: 'The Specificity Factor in Psychotherapy'. *Psychotherapy in Private Practice*, Volume 2, 1984, pp. 43-48

Lazarus, A.A. (ed.): *Casebook of Multimodal Therapy*. New York: Guilford, 1985.

Lazarus, A.A.: 'The Multimodal Approach with Adult Outpatients'. In Jacobson, N.S. (ed.): *Psychotherapists in Clinical Practice*. New York: Guilford, 1987.

Lazarus, A.A.: 'Eclecticism in Behaviour Therapy'. In Emmelkamp, P.M.G., Everaerd, W.T.A.M., Kraaimaat, F., and van Son, M.J.M. (eds.): *Advances in Theory and Practice in Behaviour Therapy*. Amsterdam: Swets & Zeitlinger, 1988.

Lazarus, A. A.: *The Practice of Multimodal Therapy*. Baltimore: Johns Hopkins University Press, 1989 (updated paperback edition).

Lazarus, A.A., and Fay, A.: 'Behavior Therapy'. In Karasu, T.B. (ed.): *The Psychiatric Therapies*. Washington, DC: American Psychiatric Association, 1984.

Lazarus, A.A., and Messer, S.B.: 'Clinical Choice Points: Behavioral versus Psychoanalytic Interventions'. *Psychotherapy*, Volume 25, 1988, pp. 59-70.

Leiblum, S.R., and Pervin, L.A. (eds.): *Principles and Practice of Sex Therapy*. New York: Guilford, 1980.

Leiblum, S.R., and Rosen, R.C. (eds.): *Sexual Desire Disorders*. New York: Guilford, 1988.

London, P.: *The Modes and Morals of Psychotherapy*. New York: Holt, Rinehart & Winston, 1964.

LoPiccolo, J., and LoPiccolo, L. (eds.): *Handbook of Sex Therapy*. New York: Plenum, 1978.

Luborsky, L., Singer, B., and Luborsky, L.: 'Comparative Studies of Psychotherapies: Is It True that "Everybody Has Won and All Must Have Prizes"?' *Archives of General Psychiatry*, Volume 32, 1975, pp. 995-1008.

Marmor, J., and Woods, S.M. (eds.): *The Interface between the Psychodynamic and Behavioral Therapies*. New York: Plenum, 1980.

Masters, W.H., and Johnson, V.E.: *Human Sexual Inadequacy*. Boston: Little, Brown, 1970.

Messer, S.B., and Winokur, M.: 'Therapeutic Change Principles: Are Commonalities More Apparent than Real?' *American Psychologist*, Volume 36, 1981, pp. 1547-1548.

Mills, H.L., Agras, W.S., Barlow, D.H., and Mills, J.R.: 'Compulsive Rituals Treated by Response Prevention'. *Archives of General Psychiatry,* Volume 28, 1973, pp. 524-529.

Norcross, J.C.(ed.): *Handbook of Eclectic Psychotherapy.* New York: Brunner/Mazel, 1986.

O'Leary, K.D., and Wilson, G.T.: *Behavior Therapy: Application and Outcome* (2nd edition). Englewood Cliffs, NJ: Prentice-Hall, 1987.

Paul, G.L.: *Insight versus Desensitization in Psychotherapy.* Stanford: Stanford University Press, 1966.

Prochaska, J.O., and DiClemente, C.C.: 'The Transtheoretical Approach'. In Norcross, J.C. (ed.): *Handbook of Eclectic Psychotherapy.* New York: Brunner/Mazel, 1986.

Rachman, S.J., and Wilson, G.T.: *The Effects of Psychological Therapy* (2nd edition). Oxford: Pergamon, 1980.

Rescorla, R.A.: 'Pavlovian Conditioning: It's Not What You Think It is'. *American Psychologist,* Volume 43, 1988, pp. 151-160.

Rush, A.J., Beck, A.T., Kovacs, M., and Hollon, S.: 'Comparative Efficacy of Cognitive Therapy and Imipramine in the Treatment of Depressed Outpatients'. *Cognitive Therapy and Research*, Volume 1, 1977, pp. 17-37.

Shapiro, D.A., and Shapiro, D.: 'Comparative Outcome Research: Methodological Implications of Meta-Analysis'. *Journal of Consulting and Clinical Psychology*, Volume 51, 1983, pp. 42-53.

Smith, M.L., Glass, G.V., and Miller, T.I.: *The Benefits of Psychotherapy*. Baltimore: Johns Hopkins University Press, 1980.

Wachtel, P.L.: *Psychoanalysis and Behavior Therapy: Toward an Integration.* New York: Basic Books, 1977.

Weed, L.L.: 'Medical Records that Guide and Teach'. *New England Journal of Medicine*, Volume 278, 1968, pp. 593-600.

Wilson, G.T.: 'How Useful is Meta-Analysis in Evaluating the Effects of Different Psychological Therapies?' *Behavioural Psychotherapy*, Volume 10, 1982, pp. 221-231.

Wilson, G.T.: 'Limitations of Meta-Analysis in the Evaluation of the Effects of Psychological Therapy'. *Clinical Psychology Review*, Volume 5, 1985, pp. 35-47.

Wilson, G.T.: 'Clinical Issues and Strategies in the Practice of Behavior Therapy'. In Wilson, G.T., Franks, C.M., Kendall, P.C., and Foreyt, J.P. (eds.): *Review of Behavior Therapy*, Volume 11, New York: Guilford, 1987.

Wilson, G.T., and Rachman, S.J.: 'Meta-Analysis and the Evaluation of Psychotherapy Outcome: Limitations and Liabilities'. *Journal of Consulting and Clinical Psychology,* Volume 51, 1983, pp. 54-64.

Wilson, G.T., and Smith, D.: 'Cognitive-Behavioral Treatment of Bulimia Nervosa'. *Annals of Behavioral Medicine*, Volume 9, 1987, pp. 12-17.

Wolpe, J., and Lazarus, A.A.: *Behavior Therapy Techniques.* New York: Pergamon, 1966.

Woolfolk, R.L., and Lehrer, P.M. (eds.): *Principles and Practice of Stress Management.* New York: Guilford, 1984.

CHAPTER 3

Why I am an Integrationist (Not an Eclectic)

Bernard D. Beitman

Department of Psychiatry, University of Missouri, USA

The author's integrative search for common factors aided by pragmatic theory is based upon several concepts: (1) counselling is a series of events through time and may be called a process; (2) general principles are to be valued over the gathering of bits of data; (3) counselling is a practical endeavour intended to help people change, and therefore (4) its theories must be connected to practical goals, requiring a giving up of major efforts to develop theories of personality and theories of the origins of psychological difficulty; (5) theories and models must be developed for the process of counselling, for factors maintaining psychological difficulty and for the process of change; and (6) emphasis must be placed on the self of the counsellor as a key component in integrative therapy. Following a personal history of factors contributing to his development as an integrationist, the author outlines his early model of the therapeutic process and moves on to several integrative principles, including: convergence among schools; the heuristic value of stages in counselling; the interpersonal nature of counselling in both its form and its major purposes; and the flexibility required by the striving for prescriptive approaches developed out of integration. Finally, the unfortunately limited value of research in integration and eclecticism is discussed.

To answer the query posed in the title, one must find acceptable definitions of integration and eclecticism. There are three major forms of integration: systematic eclecticism, common factor integration, and theoretical integration (Arkowitz, in press). My own predisposition is towards common factor integration.

Lazarus's form may be called systematic technical eclecticism, against which my form is to be contrasted. One must also offer a definition of eclecticism itself, for that concept too is to be contrasted with my own views.

First comes the problem of systematic technical eclecticism. What is it? I, like Norcross (this volume), consider it to be a form of integration. Immediately this placing of a type of 'eclecticism' under the rubric of integration distorts the apparent dualism of the title's question. The title implies a thesis and antithesis; yet, from the beginning, I dissolve the dualism by claiming that systematic technical eclecticism is part of the integration movement. Furthermore, I believe that Lazarus's BASIC ID is an excellent example of systematic technical eclecticism. Perhaps some would want the paper to end at this point, claiming no contest. In my view, however, there is much to distinguish my own form of integration from that of Lazarus, and this distinction will inform much of the body of this essay. Furthermore, my approach and that of Lazarus are each quite different from simple eclecticism, by which I mean technical selection in a haphazard, unsystematic way. While this is what I mean when I use the term 'eclecticism' without an adjective, in many respects the concept is a straw man. I believe that many counsellors possess some notions of why they do what they do but that they often have not articulated their schemas.

I do not claim to represent all integrationists, although I believe I have defined in the stages of psychotherapy (engagement, pattern search, change and termination) fundamental aspects of counselling and psychotherapeutic relationships. I am less interested in theories of personality and theories of psychopathology. I am most interested in developing a model against which idiosyncratic and school-bound approaches may be contrasted so that the stage model may be further elucidated. Through this contrast the individual approaches may also be clarified by understanding their similarities to other approaches as well as their distinctive contributions.

In line with this way of thinking is my disagreement with the premise of this book: namely, that eclecticism (or more precisely systematic technical eclecticism) and integration are fundamentally incompatible. I do not share this assumption. I see Lazarus as having made an excellent contribution to the manner in which we approach maladaptive patterns as part of the initial evaluation and the second stage of counselling. His approach, however, ignores engagement, self-observer alliance and termination among other critical concepts for the counselling relationship. In my view the concept of stages broadly encompasses the whole enterprise. Most such relationships begin with attempts to work together (engagement), efforts to define maladaptive patterns (pattern search), and attempts to initiate and maintain change (change), followed by termination. There is no mystery to this sequence. It is an outline of the steps taken when people attempt to work together to solve problems.

In this essay I pay attention to the word 'I' which is also contained in the title created by the editors. In what follows I briefly describe influences in my own history which contributed to my desire to find common factors in a variety of approaches, a desire based on the tragedies perpetrated by the despotic aspects of the world's religions and political systems. I also describe an early form of my model and the thinking that went into forming it. These sections are followed by an outline of the stages of psychotherapy, some integrative principles and comments on research in psychotherapy. First, I shall discuss some considerations preceding integrative concepts.

Considerations prior to developing integrative conceptions

Before developing concepts for integration, one must outline the framework upon which such conceptions lie.

First, what is counselling? I define individual counselling as a relationship between two people which proceeds over time and has as its purpose the psychological change for the better of the one called client. A series of events through time may be called a process. I believe in the process of psychotherapy: not only that it exists but that trusting this process, moving it along, nurturing it, and removing impediments to it, is essential to carrying out its purpose.

Second, I believe in discovering a few general principles which may be applied to a large number of situations rather than primarily gathering many bits of data which apply to limited situations. Eclectics, on the other hand, seem to gravitate primarily towards many bits of data. I search for common factors using the same basic idea I use for discovering coherence in the behaviours, thoughts and feelings of my clients. I look for repeated patterns. The word 'pattern' comes from the word 'patron' (father): it is the source of its derivatives, the children. I am guided in this search by my own personal experience, the teachings of persuasive others, and my clients. I generally consider all psychotherapists and counsellors to be practising variations on a set of basic themes. I read the self-descriptions of other psychotherapists, listen to them talk with each other in group settings and watch myself and others on videotape. I look for repeated patterns in client-counsellor interactions. These repeated patterns then emerge as fundamental aspects of psychotherapy and form the foundation of integrative psychotherapy. Lazarus seems to rely primarily on what has been shown to work and what seems scientific in the data-supported sense. As an integrationist I use research-supported findings to guide my practice, one of the most compelling of which is that technique itself accounts for a small portion of the outcome variance (Lambert, 1986). Evidence is accumulating to suggest that for specific problems like panic disorder, or depression, specific techniques are useful. But for the practising counsellor removed from the fabricated world of protocol restrictions, client and relationship variables are pre-eminent.

Third, I believe that psychotherapy is a practical endeavour with its roots in the real world, the world of action, thinking and feeling. Psychotherapy is often discussed in abstract terms but any valid conception of psychotherapy must take into consideration the bottom line: psychotherapy is intended to help people change in their lives outside the office.

Fourth, theory is alluring, attractive and necessary, but we need to determine what theories are within the province of psychotherapists. Currently there are theories of personality, theories of how people get disturbed (aetiology of psychopathology), theories of what maintains psychological difficulty and theories of change. In regard to theories of personality and theories of the aetiology of psychopathology, counselling is but one of many ways to gather

54

information to answer these questions.

Unfortunately, some counsellors have believed that they can generalise from their office experience far beyond the capabilities of these data. Genetics, brain biochemistry and childhood development research are other very important sources of data for building theories of personality and psychopathology. To ask a psychotherapist who has developed an effective technique to formulate a theory of psychopathology would be like asking a psychopharmacologist who has developed an effective medication to tell us how the brain functioned in mental illness. The ability to alleviate a mental problem must be distinguished from the ability to define the manner in which the problem originated.

Fifth, I argue for the use of both models and theories. While there is some ambiguity between these terms, they need to be differentiated. A model is an abstraction from observables; it condenses the multiple manifestations of a general phenomenon into a comprehensible configuration. A theory is primarily an attempt to explain causation, to answer the question why. Its value comes from the well-established belief that knowing the why of a phenomenon helps to change it. Psychotherapy needs models of the process of therapy (e.g. Beitman, 1987), of factors maintaining psychological difficulty (e.g. homeostasis (Pentony, 1981), and of the process of change (e.g. exposure (Barlow and Cerny, 1988; Marks, 1976) and deviation amplifying feedback (Pentony, 1981)). Psychotherapy also needs theories of the process of therapy (e.g. why is a therapeutic alliance usually necessary in psychotherapy?), theories of the maintenance of psychological difficulty (e.g. interpersonal - Strong, 1987), cognitive (Beck *et al.*, 1979), the repetition compulsion and the reinforcement properties of avoidance) and theories of the process of change (why is change so rarely sudden and permanent and so often slow with set-backs?).

Sixth, one of the more irksome aspects of Lazarus's approach is his lack of emphasis on the individual personality of the counsellor. In his view there exist no odd, strange reactions by the counsellor to the client. I use the psychodynamic term counter-transference for this ubiquitous phenomenon. In addition, an implicit assumption of multimodal therapy is that all therapists may apply BASIC ID to all clients. It does not appear to take into consideration the varying abilities, predispositions and training of the counsellors and psychotherapists. I strongly believe that the individual personality of the counsellor plays a great part in determining the form of integration selected, the strategies and tactics embraced and the success and failure of the efforts.

With that view, I turn now to my personal journey to integration. As you will see, I could not tolerate simply being pragmatic: I had to know the background, the context of my thinking. I wanted a road map that offered more than simple expediency.

Personal journey

I was born in 1942 in Detroit, Michigan, and am a son of Nazi persecution. My parents fled from Germany, my mother in 1934 and my father in 1937. Had they each not been forced to flee, they would not have been likely to meet and marry. One of my uncles was lost in the Nazi death machine. It was a cold and frightening time for my parents, huddled with friends and relatives on Kelly Street in New York City, learning more and more about deaths of fellow Jews in Germany and in other countries surrounding Germany. My grandfather had come reluctantly because he was first a German. The land on which he had lived and the town in which he had resided had been his family's before him. My father had reluctantly left with him in the beginning of 1937. I am told my grandfather stood over my crib when I was six weeks old and visiting him on Kelly Street, and rejoiced in my existence - his seed had been planted in the next land. I was the first son of the first son going back five generations.

I grew up feeling that there was great danger in the way people thought about other people's religion. I learned that the most devastating and cruel wars were fought in the name of religion. I hated the arrogance of those who killed knowing that they were right because their deity told them so.

Because of the disturbing influences of my mother on my development, I entered psychiatry with the intent stated, but unclear, that I wanted to understand her. Later I realised that I wanted to understand her influence on me and, later still, my mother in me. I began my first-year psychiatric residency eager to understand psychotherapy but found there were many schools competing for superiority, each one saying: 'I know what's right'. I met several psychoanalysts and discovered that the analytic promise of personal perfectibility was not manifested by these people. The analytic culture seemed too rule-bound; silence was idealised while action was sharply curtailed. Its inhabitants also seemed to be living out its myths. Some analysts, for example, seemed to create the Oedipal conflict in their children. I thought other psychotherapeutic schools also had useful contributions to make, just as I had come to think that each of the world's many religions had much to teach us as did each of the world's many political systems. Furthermore, each of these religions and each of these political systems might be right for specific peoples nestled in specific geographical areas, rather than one system being right for all people. I learned to be sceptical of 'revealed truth', especially when it was revealed to someone else and not to me. I was also indoctrinated into 'scientific' thinking which brought me to test ideas for myself. Sometimes I tested out in my imagination the truth value of various propositions, as Einstein had studied the laws of light and gravity by performing thought experiments using elevators hurtling through space (Holton, 1979; Shapiro, 1986).

I wanted to find what was useful from each psychotherapy school. I needed a place to stand, to get away from the conflicting ideologies and to be able to look from a distant place for what was useful about each school. I needed to be like Archimedes who said 'Give me a place to stand and I can move the world'. I needed the leverage of distance to become a self-observer for psychotherapy.

With this history so influenced by experiences demonstrating how individual and group behaviour is determined by models people hold of the world, I could not be satisfied with collecting techniques. I wanted to conceptualise psychotherapy, to develop a model of it. I wanted the model to be firmly rooted in undeniable general principles closely tied to the real-world behaviour of clients and counsellors. I also wanted it to be flexible enough to suit the special and varying circumstances of the many practitioners. I wanted to find a way to embrace both similarities and differences.

Ontogeny recapitulates phylogeny

I found a pre-Aristotelian idea to help me to integrate the various schools. In the late 19th century it was called Haekel's Law or the biogenetic law: 'ontogeny recapitulates phylogeny'. It suggested that the embryo of the individual in some way recapitulated, repeated, the historical development of the species. Following this reasoning, anatomists could become palaeontologists by studying the developing embryo to see the structural development of its predecessors. Freud used this then-popular idea as well. He thought that individual neurosis was a recapitulation of the individual's early development. This exciting notion allowed Freud to develop his theories of psychopathology and individual development from his observations in his consulting office (Sulloway, 1979). At the time I came to the idea and applied it to psychotherapy, it had come into disrepute and was being ignored by contemporary biologists. I examined some older biology texts to get ideas about it (e.g. de Beer, 1958) and gradually developed the following notion: *the individual psychotherapeutic relationship recapitulates the historical development of psychotherapy.*

Like most model builders, I tried to confirm what I had constructed. And, of course, in some general way, I was able to do so, as I applied it to the development of psychotherapy in the United States. I saw Freud as the master of the basic structure of psychotherapy, as the originator of psychotherapy as we know it now. He clarified the need to listen, and to comprehend resistance, transference, and counter-transference: each of these are ubiquitous phenomena, the importance of which varies with the client, the therapist and the nature of their relationship. Freud tried to be an observer of the psychotherapeutic process without doing much to impede it or to distort it. Of course he was observing it, therefore participating in it, therefore changing it, as suggested by the Heisenberg uncertainty principle. Freud defined the essential ingredients of the therapeutic contract and the therapeutic process.

In the 1940s Carl Rogers recognised some limitations in psychoanalysis, not the least of which were its complications. He offered a simpler approach by teaching his followers not only to listen but to let their clients know they were

58

being heard. He suggested that therapists should reflect back what they hear, using the words and the emotion of the client (Rogers, 1942). This active listening continues to be a fundamental technique for the engagement stage.

Also in the 30s and 40s, the inquiring Harry Stack Sullivan threw aside psychoanalytic silence while working with obsessives and schizophrenics. Sullivan recognised that if he did not ask any questions, he would not be able to get much clear information from these patients. He instituted the 'detailed inquiry' described in his book, *The Psychiatric Interview*, published posthumously in 1953. Sullivan helped to clarify the second stage of psychotherapy, the hallmark of which is active inquiry.

The 60s saw much transformation in psychotherapeutic technique. In 1959 Wolpe published his book on systematic desensitisation, *Psychotherapy by Reciprocal Inhibition*, which helped to revolutionise our approaches by insisting that behaviour is a critical component to therapeutic change (obvious as that may now appear). Albert Ellis in 1962 published his book, *Reason and Emotion in Psychotherapy*, emphasising the need to change cognitions. During the latter part of the 60s, Fritz Perls (e.g. Perls, 1969) rose to prominence among many counter-culture psychotherapists and moved gradually into the mainstream with his emphasis on emotion (Rice and Greenberg, 1984). In this general way, the triad of cognitions, emotion, and behaviour became the foci of change, the third stage of psychotherapy.

The 70s saw more third-party influence in psychotherapy and the need to be able to shorten the number of sessions. During that time the importance of termination and particularly of short-term therapy arose. As the 70s came to an end, two new influences appeared that were beyond what I had been thinking about in the early 70s when I was developing my model of psychotherapy. Family systems approaches have now gained a permanent place in therapeutic thinking, and the integration movement has begun to flourish. Both share the notion that the parts have some important contribution to make to the whole.

The structure of each stage

In this section I shall describe the practical details of the stage model as it has evolved since its early days (adapted from Beitman, 1987, pp. 25-30). Each stage may be seen to be composed of six elements: goals, techniques, content, resistance, transference, and counter-transference.

Goals. Goals define the boundaries of the stages. Once a goal is accomplished, the stage associated with it has been transversed. However, patient-therapist pairs must often retrace their steps to firm up their engagement or to clarify and develop patterns. The goals of engagement include the patient's development of trust and confidence in the therapist as well as a willingness to be influenced. The pattern-search goal is the development of a pattern or set of patterns that, if changed, will bring about a satisfactory psychological shift. One pattern may not be sufficient; multiple patterns may be examined and discarded before some elements that can lead to an adequate resolution are defined. The goals of change are tied to its sub-goals: the relinquishing of the old pattern, the initiating of the new, followed by practice and maintenance. The goals of termination include separating early enough to maintain goals already achieved while not extending the relationship unnecessarily.

Techniques. A wide variety of techniques may be used to accomplish the goals of each stage. Some techniques are most useful in the engagement stage (e.g. empathic reflections) and others are better suited for change (e.g. behavioural rehearsal), although many techniques may be useful in all stages. The critical question is what techniques may be most useful for accomplishing the goals of each stage in therapy, and for which clients. For patients who see themselves as students of the therapist, homework assignments may prove excellent engagement techniques.

Content. The content of therapy is the least predictable aspect of psychotherapeutic process. The wide variety of personality and psychopathology theories attests to the uncertainty therapists have in knowing what to talk about. There appear to be some general themes. Engagement is concerned with trust and competence. Pattern search is most often associated with problems in daily living surrounding interpersonal relationships. Termination is concerned with trying our new actions alone and having to say good-bye.

Resistance. During the early years of psychotherapy, when the overreaching fact was psychotherapeutic ignorance, Freud and his followers required of themselves that they listen with minimal intervention. But allowing the patient to determine much of the process while confronted with a silent listener resulted in the patients beginning to distort the person of the therapist and the process of the therapy. The therapist became more than just a physician-listener; therapy became a threatening enterprise. Patients began to subvert the therapeutic intent. They failed to free-associate, and chose to talk about inconsequential matters. The form and content of these blocks to the therapeutic flow were first thought to be great nuisances. Gradually Freud and his followers found that these resistances offered useful ways of understanding the person and his or her problems. The manner in which patients avoided problems in therapy resembled the ways in which they avoided problems outside the office.

Transference. People enter into new relationships with perceptions and attitudes derived from previous relationships. The more intimate the new relationship, the more likely it is that old, idiosyncratic attitudes will emerge. During the engagement stage, clients tend to react to the surface appearance of the therapist (age, sex, dress, manner, accent). As intimate self-revelation takes place, more stereotyped attitudes are likely to be disclosed. They may be derived from past interpersonal experiences; they may also be samples of the patient's intrapsychic dynamics. For example, a person who criticises herself for any feeling of self-compassion may react critically to demonstrations of concern by the therapist. Apparent distortions of the person of the therapist may not have their primary source in the previous experience of the client. Therapists themselves may trigger realistic responses by their own distortions of the person of the patient. For example, a sexually stimulated therapist may unwittingly induce a feeling of being helplessly in love in a susceptible client who otherwise would have remained grateful with feelings of affection.

Counter-transference. Therapists also perceive their clients in terms of their own previous relationships. In addition, patients may induce responses in susceptible therapists that are similar to reactions other people have to these patients. Once the therapist's own idiosyncratic personal responses are distinguished from the effects the patient is creating, some very useful information can emerge. First, the therapist has the opportunity to further explore the personal sources of neurotic distortions. Second, the therapist can explore the reasons for his or her own personal vulnerability to such people. Third, the therapist can gain a richer appreciation of the reasons other people have trouble relating to these patients.

Table 1 contains an outline of the stages and their basic elements.

Integrative principles

Ideally, psychotherapists should and often do operate by a limited number of flexible principles (Kelly, 1955). I will list here some of these 'good ideas' which I believe integrative therapists should incorporate.

(1) The continuing acceptance of well-defined schools is of increasingly less use, but the belief in their value will not disappear quickly. Many teachers of psychotherapy have developed review courses covering the many schools. Yet fewer practitioners will be able to wade through the volumes of texts concerning each school, and gradually they are likely to become historical anachronisms. We are witnessing much convergence and the recognition of common factors (Goldfried, 1982). Counsellors need to search for the unique contributions of each school while also taking into consideration their similarities.

Commonalities, however, may be obscured by different terms. For example, the concept of self-observation has received several other names including 'observing ego', 'self-monitoring' and 'self-reflection', each with different connotations. Another concept that has many terms is the common failure of clients to follow the therapist's expectations. Some of the terms used for this are 'resistance' or 'awareness blocks' or 'non-compliance', depending on the school of therapy. Another ubiquitous concept with different names is called

Table 1: The stages of individual psychotherapy

	Engagement	Pattern search	Change	Termination
GOALS	Trust Credibility Ground rules Self-observer alliance Motivation	To define patterns of thought, feeling and/or behaviour that, if changed, would lead to a desirable outcome.	1. Relinquish old pattern(s) 2. Initiate new pattern(s) 3. Practise new pattern(s) 4. Maintain and generalise	To separate without unnecessarily prolonging contact but with sufficient time to maintain change. To practise separation.
TECHNIQUES	Empathy Role definition Managing the contract Specialised knowledge Effective suggestions	Questionnaires Listening Questions Homework Role-playing Incongruities	Placebo response Exhortation Interpretation Reframing Modelling	Mutually agreed Patient initiates Therapist initiates
CONTENT	Presenting problems Underlying fears Distrust Therapist decisions about type of treatment	S-> O-> R Deviation amplifying feed-back Emotion Expectations Interpersonal style Intrapsychic conflict	Specifying patterns Responsibility awareness Responsibility assumption Therapist's lessons on coping and values	Separation themes Fears of relapse Mourning
RESISTANCE	To trust competence ground rules self-observer motivation	To ground rules self-observer pattern-search methods pattern-search content	To change itself Patient limitations Therapist limitations Patient-therapist impasse	Recurrence of symptoms New symptoms Impulsive behaviour (marriage, pregnancy)
TRANSFERENCE	To therapist's surface presentation(age,sex, dress,accent,race, physical attractiveness. style of therapy)	As samples of key interpersonal and key intrapsychic patterns. As products of previous therapy, expectable events of current therapy, or therapist countertransference	Fear of losing therapist Sample of behaviour to be changed and responsibility for creating it	Interpersonal attempts to hold on to or push therapist away
COUNTER-TRANSFERENCE	To patient's surface presentation (age,sex dress, accent, race, attractiveness, diagnosis)	Therapist-induced Patient-induced (informs therapist how patient affects others)	Fear of losing patient Use of understanding of how patient affects therapist in intervention (e.g. self revelation)	Interpersonal attempts to hold on to or push patient away

'exposure' in behaviour therapy, upon which it has based a great deal of its success. No matter what its form (*in-vivo*, rapid v. slow, therapist-aided v. spouse-
aided v. alone), exposure has been shown to be successful in the treatment of
phobias (Marks, 1976). More recently, it has come to be applied to panic attacks which are in part thought to be triggered by phobic reactions to internal,
somatic sensations and therefore treated with introceptive exposure (Barlow
and Cerny, 1988). Without using the term, however, exposure is also used in
other approaches. Cognitive therapists expose clients to frightening automatic
thoughts and may ask 'so what?' (Beck *et al.*, 1979). Gestalt therapists may bring
frightening feelings to awareness and ask clients to stay with them (Perls, 1969).
Psychoanalysts have long exposed their patients to forbidden impulses,
memories and images either slowly or rapidly.

(2) The stages of psychotherapy appear to be a heuristic concept for guiding us through the often tumultuous, uncertain terrain of the psychotherapeutic
experience. By knowing the current stage, one is given objectives to accomplish.
For example, with a difficult borderline patient I am currently seeing, it became
obvious that she would not develop a self-observer alliance with me and that
this resistance required investigation. Her resistance was based on her fear of
actually getting closer to me by working with me and therefore having to trust
me. She had this fear in spite of the fact that she professed great love for me
and wanted me to step out of my role and into a sexual affair with her. Trust became critical and the self-observer alliance became the focus. To move to
change immediately would have been premature.

In pattern search, one tries not only to define the patterns which are in
need of change but to define them in ways that imply change. This effort requires careful selection of terminology. The terminology should conform to the
patient's world view and world experience.

While each of the stages may have sub-stages, it is the sub-stages of change
that appear most clear. During the first sub-stage of change, clients often are
required to give up an old pattern before beginning a new one. This giving-up
sometimes involves grieving and may involve much fear. Giving up the old pat-

tern can be frightening because the new is uncertain while the old is tried and familiar and at least predictable. The second sub-stage of change requires the initiation of new ways of thinking or acting. If these ways of acting are not reinforced by the environment, one gets into trouble. After initiating new behaviours, they must be practised in positively reinforcing environments. Negative environments make successful practice difficult; couples and family therapy may then become obviously necessary.

(3) Psychotherapy is an interpersonal process. This is not to suggest that certain specific problems such as depression and panic cannot be approached in a non-interpersonal (e.g. cognitive) way (see Beck *et al.*, 1979; Barlow and Cerny, 1988). Often, however, one is using an interpersonal method to solve a problem in the person's interpersonal environment. It is also critical for therapists to recognise that patients are attempting to influence therapists as well as to acknowledge that we are trying to influence them. Acknowledging to oneself the manner in which a client is attempting to control, manipulate, and/or persuade us, tells us a great deal about the manner in which other people are indirectly asked to behave by the patient. This tendency to emit subliminal interpersonal commands has been called by many names: I prefer the term 'meta-communication' (Watzlawick *et al.*, 1967). Whatever term one prefers, it is important to recognise that we are registering both consciously and unconsciously the other person's interpersonal commands on us. Our internal responses become additional data about the client's interpersonal manoeuvres (see Strong, 1987).

(4) Counsellors must build flexibility into their approaches to their clients. This flexibility may be imagined as the counsellor's moulding around the other, a fitting with the client, rather than forcing the patient into the therapist's own theoretical bed. This flexibility may lead to our ability to prescribe certain responses for certain situations. Perhaps the most critical problem is determining the client's level of difficulty. Beutler (1983) has made a distinction between monosymptomatic and polysymptomatic presentations. For example, some people may simply have panic attacks and no personality problems or major de-

pressions. On the other hand, some people who have concurrent panic disorder and major depression are more likely to have social phobia (Stein and Uhde, 1988) and to have personality disorders - most commonly passive dependent disorder and sometimes borderline disorder. A therapist may be fooled by the presence of an apparently simple difficulty and find himself/herself entering into a very confusing and difficult arena. Making the distinction between the easier and more difficult problems will aid in determining the required flexibility.

Therapists often need to adapt to clients' vocabulary. They talk in a variety of languages and come from a variety of backgrounds. Engineers, teachers, farmers, low v. high socioeconomic groups, each may have different ways of thinking and expressing themselves to which therapists should be able to adapt.

Clients may be skilled at certain change mechanisms and not skilled at others. Some may be more attuned to focusing on emotional awareness; some may be more focused on cognitions; some may rather change behaviour first. The situation may be seen to call for certain types of responses.

(5) Psychotherapy and counselling are practised in a complex social, political and cultural context. Integrative models and theories must incorporate flexible conduits by which new ideas may be entered and tested. Rigidity to outside influence and change must be guarded against. Change must be anticipated. For example, cybernetics helped to spawn systems theory and its derivative, family systems psychotherapy. With this advance, therapists can no longer pretend that the individual psyche is separate from its interpersonal environment. The women's movement is helping to shift clinical attention from the woman as major source of difficulty to considering male authority and rationality as critical problems (Luepnitz, 1988). The length of therapy is currently strongly influenced by the willingness of society to pay for it (Kuper, 1988).

Research, integration and eclecticism

Lazarus would have us believe that his technical choices are based upon research evidence supporting the use of one approach over others. There is much in his own writing to suggest that this is not the case. One of his major claims, for instance, is that 'From a multimodal perspective ... it is therapeutically deleterious to aggrandize any particular modality - they are all important' (Lazarus, 1976, p.41). How does he know this? Upon what research other than his own careful clinical observation does he base this statement? Where are the reports that demonstrate poorer outcome when 'sensations', for example, are left out of the therapeutic content? It would take a tremendous number of clients and researchers to substantiate this claim. Furthermore, he includes among his seven modalities 'imagery', claiming by inference that the use of imagery in therapy has been well established. He recorded many useful clinical concepts in his small book on the use of imagery (Lazarus, 1977) but there is little research evidence to substantiate the use of the techniques he describes.

Research in psychotherapy has primarily investigated established approaches; it has not been the source of innovation but rather of confirmation or disconfirmation of commonly accepted techniques. As a source of technical information, the research literature functions as good criticism in that it guides the reader to focus on the optimally effective. However, there are grave limitations to relying only upon research data to guide clinical practice. Culture, clients and politics are continually changing, and therapists need new perspectives. Psychotherapy research has only reacted to what is being practised, and has only tested what is being done rather than put together new schemes or techniques.

Another problem is the research requirements demanded by research protocols. Patients must be willing to go along with what is being asked of them. Usually a good deal of co-operation and practice outside the sessions is required. Thus much sophisticated work is being done with panic disorder (e.g. Barlow and Cerny, 1988), but some patients just do not have the time, the energy or a sufficiently organised life to carry out assignments. Such clients may be termed 'non-compliant' and dropped from the protocol. Unfortunately many people in clinical practice also would be dropped from such protocols. In this way research may tell therapists about an approach that can be effective and therefore provides an ideal towards which to reach. However, other information must be added to make effective use of such clients' limited resources.

As for research that does exist, one must again fall back upon opinion to judge its clinical value. The conclusions from meta-analysis research are matters of statistical opinion. As for 'data pertaining to specific treatment of choice for a variety of problems' (the careful phrasing used by Lazarus at the end of his chapter), one cannot avoid knowing that exposure in many forms is useful for phobias. As for depressive disorders, several candidates are vying for the prizes including cognitive-behavioural (Beck *et al.*, 1979), interpersonal (Klerman *et al.*, 1984), and social skills (Hersen *et al.*, 1984). How is the clinician to choose? For obsessive-compulsive disorders, psychotherapy is difficult, with relatively low yields compared to medications which are probably the best place to start. I claim this is hardly sufficient information to guide clinical practice which includes many people with personality disorders.

Lazarus takes issue with my unproven claim that individual personality plays a great part in therapeutic choice. However, he unwittingly illustrates this point with his own approach. He wants research to guide his practice and so he says that it does. I claim that clinical experience explains a far greater portion of the variance in his choices since so many clinical problems have yet to be carefully addressed by research. In addition, several of the content areas of his BASIC ID (emotion, sensation, imagery) have not been the subject of research scrutiny from which firm conclusions can be drawn. He clearly dislikes psychoanalysis, comparing it to phrenology. How can experienced clinicians deny the existence of transference, resistance and counter-transference? Although I believe that there is much confusion, hyperbole and sophistry in psychoanalytic theory, some of its clinical insights are requisite parts of any therapeutic scheme. Although he does not mention it, I assume that Lazarus would prefer not to delve into existential concerns like death, responsibility, isolation and the

ECLECTICISM AND INTEGRATION

meaning of life (e.g. Yalom, 1980). I sometimes find these ideas useful. But Lazarus is a behaviourist by choice and therefore he chooses to ignore these non-
behavioural contributions. I consider his approach to be a behaviourally-
oriented systematic eclecticism which has made and continues to make valu-
able contributions to the movement towards psychotherapy integration.

References

Arkowitz, H.: 'The Role of Theory in Psychotherapy Integration'. *Journal of Integrative and Eclectic Psychotherapy*, Volume 8, 1989 (in press).

Barlow, D.H., and Cerny, J.A.: *Psychological Treatment of Panic*. New York:
Guilford, 1988.

Beck, A.T., Rush, A.J., Shaw, B.F., and Emery, G.: *Cognitive Therapy of Depression*. New York: Guilford, 1979.

Beitman, B.D.: *The Structure of Individual Psychotherapy*. New York: Guilford,
1987.

Beutler, L.E.: *Eclectic Psychotherapy*. New York: Pergamon, 1983.

de Beer, G.: *Embryos and Ancestors*. Oxford: Oxford University, 1958.

Goldfried, M.R. (ed.): *Converging Themes in Psychotherapy*. New York:
Springer, 1982.

Hersen, M., Bellack, A.S., Himmelhoch, J.M., and Thase, M.E.: 'Effects of Social Skill Training, Amitriptyline and Psychotherapy in Unipolar Depressed
Women'. *Behavior Therapy*, Volume 15, 1984, pp. 21-40.

Holton, G.: 'What Precisely is "Thinking?"': Einstein's Answer'. In French, A.P.
(ed.): *Einstein: a Centenary Volume*. Cambridge, Massachusetts: Harvard
University Press, 1979.

Kelly, G.A.: *The Psychology of Personal Constructs* (2 volumes). New York:
W.W. Norton, 1955.

Klerman, G.L., Weissman, M.M., Rounsaville, B.J., and Chevron, E.S.: *Interpersonal Psychotherapy of Depression*. New York: Basic Books, 1984.

Kuper, T.: *Ending Therapy: The Meaning of Termination*. New York: New York
University Press, 1988.

Lambert, M.: 'Some Implications of Psychotherapy Outcome Research for
Eclectic Psychotherapy'. *International Journal of Eclectic Psychotherapy*, Volume 5 No. 1, 1986, pp. 16-46.

Lazarus, A.A.: *Multimodal Behavior Therapy*. New York: Springer, 1976.

Lazarus, A.A.: *In the Mind's Eye*. New York: Rawson, 1977.

Luepnitz, D.A.: *The Family Interpreted: Feminist Theory in Clinical Practice*. New York: Basic Books, 1988.

Marks, I.M.: 'The Current Status of Behavioral Psychotherapy'. *American Journal of Psychiatry*, Volume 133, 1976, pp. 253-261.

Pentony, P.: *Models of Influence in Psychotherapy*. New York: Free Press, 1981.

Perls, F.: *Gestalt Therapy Verbatim*. Lafayette, California: Real People Press, 1969.

Rogers, C.R.: *Counseling and Psychotherapy*. Boston: Houghton Mifflin, 1942.

Rice, L.N., and Greenberg, L.S.(eds.): *Patterns of Change*. New York: Guilford, 1984.

Shapiro, S.I.: 'Thought Experiments for Psychotherapists'. *International Journal of Eclectic Psychotherapy*. Volume 5, 1986, pp. 69-70.

Stein, M.B., and Uhde, T.W.: 'Panic Disorder and Major Depression'. *Psychiatric Clinics in North America*, Volume 11 No. 2, 1988.

Strong, S.R.: 'Interpersonal Theory as a Common Language for Psychotherapy'. *Journal of Integrative and Eclectic Psychotherapy*, Volume 6, 1987, pp.173-183.

Sulloway, F.S.: *Freud, Biologist of the Mind: Beyond the Psychoanalytic Legend*. New York: Basic Books, 1979.

Watzlawick, P., Beavin, J.H., Jackson, D.D., and Fisch, R.: *Pragmatics of Human Communication*. New York: Norton, 1967.

Yalom, I.: *Existential Psychotherapy*. New York: Basic Books, 1980.

CHAPTER 4

Integration and Eclecticism in Counselling and Psychotherapy: Cautionary Notes

Stanley B Messer

Graduate School of Applied and Professional Psychology

Rutgers State University of New Jersey, USA

Obstacles on the path to integration and eclecticism are illustrated in three realms of endeavour: the therapeutic relationship, the constitution of knowledge, and visions of reality. The strands of three major systems of psychotherapy - the psychoanalytic, the behavioural and the humanistic - are examined as to the desired nature of the therapist-client relationship, their sources and understanding of data, and the worldviews they encompass from among the romantic, ironic, tragic and comic. Differences among these theories of psychotherapy are seen to limit the possibilities for integration and eclecticism. This conclusion is tempered, however, by a recognition of the value of each approach assimilating some views of the others in a considered way.

On the face of it , it is hard to argue with an attitude of eclecticism, at least as it is defined by *The College Dictionary*: to wit, 'not following any one system, as of philosophy, medicine, etc., but selecting and using what are considered the best elements of all systems'. After all, why not employ what is best rather than what, by implication, is second best? Similarly positive is the definition of 'integrate' given by *Webster's Dictionary*: namely, 'to make whole or complete by ad-

71

ding or bringing together parts'. Why select an incomplete or partial theory or psychotherapy if one can have a unified whole? Besides, there is safety and comfort in numbers. Supporting the allure and strength of eclecticism, surveys indicate that the number of counselling and clinical psychologists who regard themselves as eclectic (30% to 55%) far exceeds the number of adherents to any single school of psychotherapy (Garfield and Kurtz, 1976; 1977; Kelly, 1961; Norcross, 1986; Smith, 1982). To offer one more indicator of the rise of eclecticism and integration, there is now both a Society for the Exploration of Psychotherapy Integration and a *Journal of Integrative and Eclectic Psychotherapy* to serve as forums for the discussion and dissemination of ideas and research in this area.

Notwithstanding the potential strengths and advantages of eclecticism and integration, my object in this article is to offer some cautionary notes, and to point to the kind of choices and trade-offs such an approach entails. In doing so I will bring together and condense some of the arguments and outlooks that I have presented in various articles and chapters over the past ten years, and will provide references for the reader interested in a fuller treatment of the subject.

The challenge of integration and eclecticism can be taken up at different levels of abstraction, including the clinical, the methodological, and the metatheoretical. Let us begin with the clinical.

Eclecticism/integration and the therapeutic relationship

Although it is possible to select any one of a number of clinical issues or practices to illustrate and discuss the difficulties of eclecticism and integration, the nature of the relationship between therapist and client is particularly suitable because it is of paramount importance for all therapies. Can one be integrative or eclectic in the kind of relationship that one establishes in counselling or psychotherapy without undermining the very premises of the theory of therapy upon which one draws? To demonstrate the barriers faced by the eclectic or integrationist, let us examine the nature of this special relationship as it is viewed, in turn, by the psychoanalyst, the behaviour therapist, and the person-centred counsellor.

The psychoanalytic perspective. In differentiating between the real relationship, the working alliance and the transferential relationship, Greenson (1967; 1971) systematised the psychoanalytic theory of the therapist-client relationship. The *real relationship* is a genuine person-to-person relationship between client and therapist, which can be characterised as appropriate, realistic, objective and authentic. To give an example of a therapist responding as a real person: if a client has just been involved in an automobile accident or has suffered a grievous loss, the therapist does not remain silent (Stone, 1961) - that would be a breach of the natural, human and empathic attitude, which optimally should characterise all relationships, including that between client and therapist.

The *working alliance* constitutes the co-operative and willing proclivities of the client to overcome his or her neurotic problems, and to achieve the insights that analytic therapy has to offer. It is the unwritten and often unspoken contract between therapist and client to co-operate on a difficult but, it is hoped, rewarding joint enterprise each with his or her own prescribed role. Even while the client is experiencing disturbing sexual, aggressive or dependency fantasies towards the therapist, the working alliance allows the client to continue co-operating to achieve the aims of therapy by means of the implicitly agreed-upon analytic method of telling all and exploring all. The client is allied with the therapist in this endeavour, and without such a working agreement, therapy flounders. It has also been noted that both the real relationship and the working alliance are affected by the state of the transference, and thus are not completely separable from it (Frieswyck *et al.*, 1986).

Note that the working alliance differs from the real relationship in important respects. In typical interpersonal relations there is a mutuality of need gratification such that each person satisfies the other in a rather direct way. In the working alliance, the client agrees, whether it is verbalised or not, to forego usual gratification in order that the therapist will be in a better position to increase insight into his or her needs and problems (Weiner, 1975). Questions may not be answered, requests may be denied, silence may be observed, all of which would put a marked strain on a normal interaction between two people, but which are tolerated by the client through the medium of the working alliance in the interest of the treatment goals.

Finally, there is the *transference relationship*, the hallmark of psychoanalysis and its unique contribution to the understanding of the therapist-client relationship. Whereas the real relationship and the working alliance are sensible, adaptive and reality-oriented, the transference relationship is the inappropriate and irrational way in which the client experiences the therapist. It is based on the client's experience of earlier relationships and, in this sense, it is a displacement of feelings, attitudes and impulses from the past on to the figure of the analyst. In its classical guise, the rationale for the relative neutrality and anonymity of the therapist is precisely that it allows for the client's projected distortions to be played out in the transference. These distortions can be interpreted in a convincing way because of the nebulous stimulus which the analyst presents. This ambiguity is enhanced, for example, by the client lying on the couch with the analyst out of sight, by the office being unrevealing of personal tastes, by the therapist not self-disclosing, and by his or her avoiding any relationship or contact with the client outside of the office, even of a casual nature. It is this emphasis that has made the advocacy of a real relationship within the psychoanalytic treatment context so controversial (see Brenner, 1979; Kanzer, 1981; Langs, 1976). For a further elaboration of the development of these concepts in psychoanalytic therapy, see Messer (1988).

The behavioural perspective. The hallmark of the behavioural approach to the therapist-client relationship is the therapist as educator. Behaviour therapy, after all, is based primarily on principles of social learning and it is consistent with such a viewpoint to stress the role of the therapist as teacher, persuader and environmental arranger. Also highlighted is the technical role of the therapist in his or her capacity as deliverer of intervention strategies (Wilson *et al.*, 1984). In fact, behaviour therapy is distinguished from other therapies in part by its claim that relationship and intervention strategies can be discussed separately (Linehan, 1988). Lazarus's initial treatment of a client with a handwashing compulsion and agoraphobia illustrates the behaviour therapist's role (Lazarus and Messer, 1988). As part of a strategy for helping the client gain control over her compulsion, he told her that she could wash her hands no more than four times a day, shower only twice a day and so on, to which she agreed. In connection with her agoraphobia, she was given information about the value of deep muscle relaxation, imaginal and *in vivo* exposure and response prevention. Lazarus also taught her how to relax and gave her audiotapes which promoted an inner sense of calm. In the terms used above, the working alliance was fostered, the real relationship was acknowledged, but the transference relationship was ignored. (In his later treatment of this woman, conducted according to the principles of 'multi-modal' therapy, Lazarus did address the transference). Before discussing the implications of the differences between behavioural and psychoanalytic approaches for integration or eclecticism, let us turn to the person-centred view.

The person-centred perspective. In contrast to its status in behaviour therapy, the relationship between therapist and client is at the epicentre of person-centred therapy. The relationship conditions that Rogers (1957) laid down are considered to be the necessary and sufficient conditions for growth and personality change in therapy. These include empathy, unconditional positive regard or non-possessive warmth, and congruence or genuineness. 'If experienced by the client as they are intended by the therapist, they constitute a powerful stimulus for the client's exploration and feeling of increasing regard for his or her own world of experience' (Raskin, 1985, p. 163). Unconditional positive regard involves prizing the person as he or she is as a unique human being. Empathy entails a moment-to-moment tracking of the person's reality and experience, enabling the client to do likewise (Rice, 1988). Congruence requires that the therapist be accurately aware of his or her own feelings and be willing to share them when appropriate. In Greenson's scheme referred to above, the relationship is viewed at all times as real, not transferential. A working alliance is seen to develop as a natural consequence of the empathy, prizing and genuineness of the therapist.

Implications for eclecticism and integration. Now suppose that psychoanalytic therapists, in the spirit of integration, wish to introduce behavioural techniques into therapy. In so doing, are they not also assuming the directly educative stance of behaviour therapists? Viewed psychoanalytically, the authoritative and didactic stance may lead clients to comply with therapists' suggestions in an effort to please them, and thereby, to a curtailment of freely expressed fears and wishes. In Berman's (1985, p. 57) experience, when dynamic therapists set themselves up as actual authorities, this led to anxieties which were harder to verbalise (e.g. when the therapist's advice had not been followed, or had been followed but proved to be misguided, etc.). In this way the flow of associations becomes more constrained, producing less rich material for analysis (Messer and Winokur, 1980).

Likewise, the greater self-disclosure of person-centred therapists will muddy the transferential waters, and their greater warmth may inhibit clients' ability to express negative feelings. Viewing all three therapies together, how can one be, simultaneously, neutral in the service of transference, real and genuine in the service of authenticity, and didactic in the service of guiding the client, when each role interferes to some extent with the other? In this connection, Rice (1988) has pointed out that the emphasis on transference interpretation in psychoanalytic therapy would dilute the focus on and power of the real relationship fostered in person-centred therapy. Both behavioural and psychoanalytic therapy, in their own way, place therapists in the role of experts, whereas person-centred therapy views clients as the experts on their own experience. The point is that the kind of relationship fostered within one theoretical framework is not readily integrated with that of another.

To stress the limits of integration, however, is not to say that there is no shared arena or that each approach has not borrowed eclectically from the others. That is, one need not take an all-or-none approach in these matters. For example, within the branch of psychoanalysis known as 'self psychology', therapists have become more involved participants in the relationship. In the spirit of person-centred therapy, they are likely to show more active caring, empathy and support, especially when working with more seriously disturbed clients.

Similarly, cognitive-behaviour therapists like Arnkoff (1982) and Linehan (1988) have stressed that behaviour therapists cannot ignore the interpersonal elements of therapy, and that a warm and caring relationship in an atmosphere of trust is an important facet of behaviour therapy too. As we can see, there is a delicate balancing act involved in trying to integrate different relationship modes. Clinicians are well advised to remain aware of the ways in which the nature of the relationship they foster can help or hinder both the kind of process they are fostering in therapy and, ultimately, the kind of client change they are attempting to bring about.

Eclecticism/integration and methods of knowing

In order to integrate the different therapies, there must be some acceptance of the different sorts and sources of data on which each therapy relies as an evidential base. This is much more problematic than one might suppose. One has only to pick up an issue each of the *International Journal of Psychoanalysis, Behavior Therapy, Journal of Humanistic Psychology*, and *Review of Existential and Phenomenological Psychology* to realise the vastly different ways in which the data of human behaviour are collected, analysed and interpreted, and so to appreciate fully the obstacles to integration. There is a great disparity in method displayed in these published articles (Messer, 1986a). The dichotomy can be described as a scientific v. humanistic outlook in which adherents of the scientific outlook rely on observation, laboratory studies, elementism and objectivism leading to universal or nomothetic laws, while adherents of the humanistic perspective prefer phenomenological description, case study, holism and subjectivism resulting in contextually meaningful, idiographic statements. Kimble (1984) and Krasner and Houts (1984) have demonstrated, in fact, the sharply divergent discipline-related value systems and epistemological stances of different groups of psychologists.

To illustrate this, a phenomenological psychologist, in the humanistic tradition, might study a subject of interest through the description of experience as it is lived, introspective reflection, metaphorical comparison, and the way in which the various observations cohere. A psychoanalyst studying the same phenomenon might employ free association and dream analysis in a small number of carefully selected cases studied in depth to assess unconscious or implicit determinants, and then place them within a holistic, structural-developmental framework (Messer, 1985). A behaviourist would formulate a hypothesis, construct an experiment, analyse the results using a variety of statistical measures, and tie the finding to some form of learning theory.

To state this difference in another way, phenomenological and psychoanalytic psychologists are often adherents of a hermeneutic or interpretive outlook which emphasises meanings as experienced by individuals whose activities are rooted in given socio-historical settings. The hermeneutic approach insists upon the inseparability of fact and value, detail and context, and observation and theory. Methodological hermeneutics emphasises qualitative description, analogical understanding and narrative modes of exposition (Messer *et al.*, 1988). The narrative understanding arrived at is evaluated by its logical consistency, its coherence and by its configuration - the harmony of the parts with the whole. Psychoanalytic method, for example, emphasises inner consistency and a network of converging observations that determine the form of psychoanalytic interpretations.

While this approach may be agreeable to and considered legitimate by psychoanalytic and humanistic practitioners of the existential and phenomenological variety, it will leave behaviour therapists cold. Where, they may ask, is the careful experiment with its specified procedures, operationalised variables, and controls? Where is the order, lawfulness and causality of normative science? Where are the goals of prediction and control, and where are the behavioural science rules of reliability, validity and replicability (Messer and Winokur, 1984)? As Franks (1984) has pointed out in discussing the problems of psychotherapy integration: 'It might also be difficult in actual practice for behaviour therapists to abandon their customary objective approach to all patients and proceed largely in terms of the more subjective, intuitive feeling and interpretive style of the psychodynamic clinician' (p.241).

What I wish to emphasise here is that the choice of method of investigation and analysis will be a powerful determinant of the outcome of studies conducted by adherents of one or another approach. Whose results - on which one bases one's applied work in psychology - is one to believe or take seriously? One's theoretical leanings and epistemological tastes will surely play a major role in answering this question. Is it possible, in the spirit of integration, to accept both empiricist and interpretive outlooks? There are those who believe so. Barratt (1976) writes that psychology should involve an interplay between hermeneutic and naturalistic discourse. This complementarity has not yet been achieved, but if and when it is, the outlook for integrating therapies and establishing eclectic systems of therapy will improve.

Eclecticism/integration and visions of reality

In addition to the clinical and methodological obstacles to integration and eclecticism, one can discern in the underlying visions of life that each therapy encompasses, some further barriers and possibilities (Messer and Winokur, 1980; 1984; 1986). In this section I will draw on the distinctions made by Northrop Frye (1957; 1965) in this categorisation of different forms of literature, which have been applied to psychoanalysis by Schafer (1976). In doing so, I will illustrate the intersection of these visions with psychoanalytic, behavioural and humanistic therapies, and then draw out the implications for integration and eclecticism.

The romantic vision. From the romantic viewpoint, life is an adventure or quest with the person as hero. 'It is a drama of the triumph of good over evil, of virtue over vice, of light over darkness, and of the ultimate transcendence of man over the world in which he was imprisoned by the Fall' (White, 1973, p. 9). The romantic vision emphasises exploration and conquest of the unknown, the mysterious, the irrational. It is more the world as we would like it to be than the world as we find it.

Humanistic therapists, such as Maslow (1971) and Rogers (1961), view life primarily as an adventuresome quest. In emphasising people's potential for continued psychological growth, their willingness to take risks, and the ability to self-actualise, humanistic therapies are operating with a romantic outlook. Rogers, in fact, claims that we are born with an 'organismic valuing' process that allows us to appreciate and strive for that which is life-enhancing.

Psychoanalytic therapy also partakes of the romantic vision but with a different emphasis. In stressing an exploration of that which is unconscious, irrational and unknown, psychoanalysts are influenced by the romantic attitude. Psychoanalysis is also viewed as a journey, a quest for redemption. The therapeutic process encourages a regression away from everyday reality and into the world of dreams, free associations, and fantasies. Unlike humanistic therapy, however, it envisions more obstacles *en route* and is much less optimistic about the possibilities for ultimate self-actualisation and liberation.

In contrast to both psychoanalytic and humanistic therapies, the behaviour therapies are much more reality-oriented and practical than they are romantic. While behaviour therapists may hold an attitude of curiosity and openness to the unexpected and the unknown, exploration of irrational fantasies is not encouraged in behaviour therapy. Rather, problems are operationally defined, carefully measured on objective scales, and pragmatically treated. In some forms of cognitive behaviour therapy, for example, irrational thoughts are disputed rather than explored (e.g. Ellis and Grieger, 1977). The romantic notion of the quest - so prominent in psychoanalytic and humanistically oriented therapy - is almost entirely absent in behaviour therapy.

The ironic vision. In some ways, the ironic perspective represents the flip-side of the romantic vision. It is an attitude of detachment, of keeping things in perspective, of recognising that there is another side of the coin. It challenges our beliefs, traditions and (romantic) illusions. 'The ironic perspective in analytic work results in the analysand's coming to see himself or herself as being less in certain emotional respects than was initially thought - less, that is, than the unconscious ideas of omnipotence and omniscience imply' (Schafer, 1976, p.52). Interestingly, humanistic therapy is linked in a dialectical fashion to psychoanalysis in that it results in clients seeing themselves and life's possibilities as *more* than they initially thought.

Psychoanalytic therapists adopt the ironic attitude in therapy when they take a position of relative detachment (Stein, 1985). They do so in order to detect the flip-side of the client's utterances and behaviour: the hidden meanings, contradictions, and paradoxes - how cheerfulness may cover sadness, and well-wishing, murderous thoughts. By contrast, behaviour therapists and humanistic therapists are more apt to be friendly, self-disclosing, transparent and affectively expressive, which may lessen the possibility of discerning irony. Behaviour therapists are also more likely to accept client complaints at face value, including their stated therapeutic objectives (Wilson and O'Leary, 1980), and humanistic therapists tend to accept most client feelings as authentic expression. It is the essence of the ironic posture to take nothing for granted and, in this sense, such accepting attitudes are a breach of the ironic position. Note how these differences stand in the way of fully integrating these therapies.

The tragic vision. The tragic and ironic visions are linked insofar as they both include a distrust of romantic illusions and happy endings in life. Tragedy, however, unlike irony, involves commitment. In a tragic drama, the hero has acted with purpose, and in so doing, has committed an act causing shame or guilt. He or she suffers by virtue of the conflict between passion and duty and, after considerable inner struggle, arrives at a state of greater self-knowledge. Within the tragic vision, life's limitations are accepted - not all is possible or redeemable. The clock cannot be turned back, death cannot be undone, man's nature cannot be radically perfected.

In viewing people as fundamentally good, innocent and unfallen (e.g. Rogers, 1961), the beliefs of humanistic therapy fly in the face of the tragic vision. To posit an inborn 'striving toward superiority or perfection' (Adler, 1927) or to emphasise the possibility of 'unselfish love' and 'unbiased understanding' (Maslow, 1962) is to accentuate the romantic and to downplay the tragic. Psychoanalysis, by contrast, views Man as caught within early fixations which result from our sexual and aggressive nature and the conflicts these give rise to. The psychoanalytic therapist believes 'that suffering while learning and changing cannot usually be avoided, nor can the analysand realize himself or herself most fully and resume growth in the absence of adversity and deprivation' (Schafer, 1976, p.42). Behaviour therapy, by emphasising learning through modelling and reinforcement, allows for greater optimism regarding people's ability to change. Similarly, cognitive behaviour therapists, in focusing on the correction of irrational cognitive constructions and attributions, imply a malleable and readily improvable subject. The client is helped to change his or her behaviour or thoughts rather than to reach an inner reconciliation based on self-knowledge as in psychoanalytic therapy.

The comic vision. Whereas in tragedy things go from bad to worse, in comedy the direction of events is from bad to better or even best. Although there are obstacles and struggles, they are overcome and there is a reconciliation between hero and antagonist, between the person and his or her world. Harmony and unity, progress and happiness prevail. Note that the conflicts portrayed in a comedy are ones between people and the unfortunate situation in which they find themselves, and not the kind of inner struggles or implacable oppositions encountered in dramatic tragedy.

In behaviour therapy, as in the comic outlook, conflict is often ascribed to external situations or forces which can be mastered through the application of behavioural principles. A phobia of crossing bridges, or a complaint of lack of assertiveness, is approached head-on with a spirit of optimism and laboratory-tested techniques from the behavioural repertoire. By contrast, struggles over separation issues symbolically expressed in difficulty crossing a bridge, or over fear of aggressive impulses in the unassertive client, are explored by the psychoanalyst not only with the goal of their remediation (psychoanalysis does have some comic thrust), but with the view that increased consciousness of one's condition is itself worthwhile.

Humanistic therapists do not strive for happy endings in quite the way behaviour therapists do, nor are they basically as contemplative about inevitable warring and discordant factions of the mind as are psychoanalysts. But they do emphasise the substantial possibilities for gratifying impulses which Kris (1937) has described as an essential aspect of the comic view. For them, a freer, more joyful, laughter-filled existence is attainable. The true self one comes to know in humanistic therapy is not one fraught with struggle, nor is it one seeking reduction of tension, but rather it is an authentic self, free of conditions of worth, in touch with its natural, organismic valuing, and satisfied with life's enormous possibilities for self-enhancement. Insofar as the humanistic therapist's job is to penetrate the false self, and reveal the good, innocent, unfallen romantic beneath, it partakes of the comic vision.

Conclusion and possibilities

The major thrust of the comparisons just drawn is to illustrate that the effort to integrate or draw together eclectically the different strands of the several therapies will inevitably compromise one or another of the visions they encompass. It is not simple stubbornness or inflexibility that arouses opposition to eclecticism or integration. Rather, it is the deeply-held beliefs about what constitutes human nature, what the proper goals are for psychotherapy according to the therapy's visions, and the kind of therapeutic process most likely to bring about these goals.

Nevertheless, a certain degree of integration, borrowing and assimilating of ideas from other therapies is probably inevitable and is, in any case, desirable (Messer, 1986b). For example, the variants of psychoanalysis such as ego psychology, neo-Freudianism and brief dynamic therapy (Winokur *et al.*,1981) bring psychoanalytic therapy closer in its outlook and practice to both behaviour therapy and humanistic therapy. In emphasising the sociocultural influences and the power of the ego v. the immutable drives, and the curative power of the client-therapist relationship v. self-knowledge through interpretation, the full force of the tragic viewpoint is muted. Behaviour therapy has become more eclectic by bringing cognitive, affective and even unconscious factors into its purview (Bowers and Meichenbaum, 1984; Mahoney, 1980). The attractiveness of eliminating problems like phobias, compulsions and headaches in a rather straightforward way is traded off for a more complicated and subjective view of client problems. Similarly, humanistic therapy has been broadened and deepened by the inclusion of cognitive concepts (Wexler and Rice, 1974), and interpretation (Ivey and Simek-Downing, 1980), even while accurate empathy remains the *sine qua non* of at least person-centred therapy.

Our field advances through discourse and dialogue among proponents of different, even opposing, viewpoints. I cannot imagine all psychologists sharing but one theoretical or therapeutic outlook. That would simply reflect a failure of imagination and ultimately would have a deadening effect on the therapeutic enterprise. However, not to learn from others, and not to adjust and change our outlook at all, is equally stultifying. In this sense, the efforts at integration and eclecticism constitute a welcome alternative to entrenched schoolism and a reminder that we must constantly search for better ways to address the needs of those we serve.

References

Adler, A.: *The Practice and Theory of Individual Psychology*. New York: Harcourt, Brace & World, 1927.

Arnkoff, D.B.: 'Common and Specific Factors in Cognitive Therapy'. In Lambert M.J. (ed.): *Psychotherapy and Patient Relationships*. Homewood, Illinois: Dorsey, 1982.

Barratt, B.B.: 'Freud's Psychology as Interpretation'. In Shapiro, T. (ed.): *Psychoanalysis and Contemporary Science*, Volume 5. New York: International Universities Press, 1976.

Berman, E.: 'Eclecticism and its Discontents'. *International Journal of Psychiatry and Related Sciences*, Volume 22, 1985, pp. 51-60.

Bowers, K., and Meichenbaum, D. (eds.): *The Unconscious Reconsidered*. New York: Wiley, 1984.

Brenner, C.: 'Working Alliance, Therapeutic Alliance, and Transference'. *Journal of the American Psychoanalytic Association*, Volume 27, (Supplement), 1979, pp. 137-158.

Ellis, A., and Grieger, R. (eds.): *Handbook of Rational-Emotive Therapy*. New York: Springer, 1977.

Franks, C.: 'On Conceptual and Technical Integrity in Psychoanalysis and Behavior Therapy: Two Fundamentally Incompatible Systems'. In Arkowitz, H., amd Messer, S.B. (eds.): *Psychoanalytic Therapy and Behavior Therapy: Is Integration Possible?* New York: Plenum, 1984.

Frieswyck, S.H., Allen, J.G., Colson, D.B., Coyne, L., Gabbard, G.O., Horwitz, L., and Gavin, N.: 'Therapeutic Alliance: its Place as a Process and Outcome Variable in Dynamic Psychotherapy Research'. *Journal of Consulting and Clinical Psychology*, Volume 54, 1986, pp. 32-38.

Frye, N.: *Anatomy of Criticism*. New York: Athaneum, 1957.

Frye, N.: *A Natural Perspective: the Development of Shakespearean Comedy and Romance*. New York: Columbia University Press, 1985.

Garfield, S.L., and Kurtz, R.: 'Clinical Psychologists in the 1970's. *American Psychologist*, Volume 31, 1976, pp. 1-9.

Garfield, S.L., and Kurtz, R.: 'A Study of Eclectic Views'. *Journal of Consulting and Clinical Psychology*, Volume 45, 1977, pp. 78-83.

Greenson, R.R.: *The Technique and Practice of Psychoanalysis*, Volume 1. New York: International Universities Press, 1967.

Greenson, R.R.: 'The "Real" Relationship between the Patient and the Psychoanalyst'. In Kanzer, M. (ed.): *The Unconscious Today*. New York: International Universities Press, 1971.

Ivey, A.E., and Simek-Downing, L.: *Counseling and Psychotherapy: Skills and Practice*. Englewood Cliffs, NJ: Prentice Hall, 1980.

Kanzer, M.: 'Freud's "Analytic Pact": the Standard Therapeutic Alliance'. *Journal of the American Psychoanalytic Association*, Volume 29, 1981, pp. 69-87.

Kelly, E.L.: 'Clinical Psychology - 1960: Report of Survey Findings'. *Newsletter, Division of Clinical Psychology*, Winter 1961, pp. 1-11.

Kimble, G.A.:'Psychology's Two Cultures'. *American Psychologist*, Volume 39, 1984, pp. 833-839.

Krasner, L., and Houts, A.C.: 'A Study of the "Value" Systems of Behavioral Scientists'. *American Psychologist*, Volume 39, 1984, pp. 840-850.

Kris, E.: 'Ego Development and the Comic'. In *Psychoanalytic Explorations in Art*. New York: International Universities Press, 1937.

Langs, R.: *The Therapeutic Interaction: a Critical Overview and Synthesis*. New York: Jason Aronson, 1976.

Lazarus, A.A., and Messer, S.B.: 'Clinical Choice Points: Behavioural versus Psychoanalytic Interventions'. *Psychotherapy*, Volume 25, 1988, pp. 59-70.

Linehan, M.: 'Perspectives on the Interpersonal Relationship in Behavior Therapy'. *Journal of Integrative and Eclectic Psychotherapy*, Volume 7, 1988, pp. 278-290.

Mahoney, M.J.: 'Psychotherapy and the Structure of Personal Revolutions'. In Mahoney, M.J.(ed.): *Psychotherapy Process: Current Issues and Future Directions*. New York: Plenum 1980.

Maslow, A.H.: 'Some Basic Propositions of a Growth and Self-Actualization Psychology'. In *Perceiving, Behaving, Becoming: a New Focus for Education*. Washington, DC: Association for Supervision and Curriculum Development, 1962.

Maslow, A.H.: *The Farther Reaches of Human Nature*. New York: Viking, 1971.

Messer, S.B.: 'Choice of Method is Value-Laden Too'. *American Psychologist*, Volume 40, 1985, pp. 1414-1415.

Messer, S.B.: 'Eclecticism im Psychotherapy: Underlying Assumptions, Problems and Tradeoffs'. In Norcross, J.C. (ed.): *Handbook of Eclectic Psychotherapy*. New York: Brunner/Mazel, 1986(a).

Messer, S.B.: 'Behavioral and Psychoanalytic Perspectives at Therapeutic Choice Points'. *American Psychologist*, Volume 41, 1986(b), pp. 1261-1272.

Messer, S.B.: 'Psychoanalytic Perspectives on the Therapist-Client Relationship'. *Journal of Integrative and Eclectic Psychotherapy*, Volume 7, 1988, pp. 278-290.

Messer, S.B., and Winokur, M.: 'Some Limits to the Integration of Psychoanalytic and Behavior Therapy'. *American Psychologist*, Volume 35, 1980, pp. 818-827.

Messer, S.B., and Winokur, M.: 'Ways of Knowing and Visions of Reality in Psychoanalytic Therapy and Behavior Therapy'. In Arkowitz, H., and Messer, S.B., (eds.): *Psychoanalytic Therapy and Behavior Therapy: Is Integration Possible?*. New York: Plenum, 1984.

Messer, S.B., and Winokur, M.: 'Eclecticism and the Shifting Visions of Reality in Three Systems of Psychotherapy'. *International Journal of Eclectic Psychotherapy*, Volume 5, 1986, pp. 115-124.

Messer, S.B., Sass, L.A., and Woolfolk, R.L. (eds.): *Hermeneutics and Psychological Theory*. New Brunswick, NJ: Rutgers University Press, 1988.

Norcross, J.C. (ed.): *Handbook of Eclectic Psychotherapy*. New York: Brunner/Mazel, 1986.

Raskin, N.J.: 'Client-Centred Therapy'. In Lynn, S.J., and Garske, J.P. (eds.): *Contemporary Psychotherapies*. Columbus, Ohio: Merrill, 1985.

Rice, L.: 'Integration and the Client-Centered Relationship'. *Journal of Integrative and Eclectic Psychotherapy*, Volume 7, 1988, pp. 291-302.

Rogers, C.: 'The Necessary and Sufficient Conditions of Therapeutic Personality Change'. *Journal of Consulting Psychology*, Volume 21, 1957, pp. 95-103.

Rogers, C.: *On Becoming a Person*. Boston: Houghton Mifflin, 1961.

Schafer, R.: *A New Language for Psychoanalysis*. New Haven: Yale University Press, 1961.

Smith, D.: 'Trends in Counseling and Psychotherapy'. *American Psychologist*, Volume 37, 1982, pp. 802-809.

Stein, M.H.: 'Irony in Psychoanalysis'. *Journal of the American Psychoanalytic Association*, Volume 33, 1985, pp.35-37.

Stone, L.: *The Psychoanalytic Situation*. New York: International Universities Press, 1961.

Weiner, I.B.: *Principles of Psychotherapy*. New York: Wiley, 1975.

Wexler, D.A., and Rice, L.N.: *Innovations in Client-Centered Therapy*. New York: Wiley, 1974.

White, H.: *Metahistory*. Baltimore, Maryland: Johns Hopkins University Press, 1973.

Wilson, G.T., and O'Leary, K.D.: *Principles of Behavior Therapy*. Englewood Cliffs, NJ: Prentice-Hall, 1980.

Wilson, G.T., Franks, C.M., Brownell, K.D., and Kendall, P.C.: *Annual Review of Behavior Therapy: Theory and Practice*, Volume 9. New York: Guilford, 1984.

Winokur, M., Messer, S.B., and Schacht, T.: 'Contributions to the Theory and Practice of Short-Term Dynamic Psychotherapy'. *Bulletin of the Menninger Clinic*, Volume 45, 1981, pp. 125-142.